QUILTMAKER'S GUIDE:

Basics & Beyond

QUILTMAKER'S GUIDE:

Basics & Beyond

by

Carol Doak

American Quilter's Society

P. O. Box 3290 • Paducah, KY 42002-3290

COVER QUILT

FOREVER FRIENDS is a 73" x 73" quilted wallhanging designed and made in 1990 by Carol Doak and Sherry Reis as a tribute to their deep friendship, which began in a beginning quilt class over a decade ago. The center of the quilt is based on a papercutting design by Alison Cosgrove Tanner, used with her permission, and is totally pieced. The traditional patchwork blocks which surround it were chosen because each one had some relevance to this special friendship.

Library of Congress Cataloging-in-Publication Data

Doak, Carol.
    Quiltmaker's guide: basics & beyond/by Carol Doak.
      p. cm.
    Includes bibliographical references and index.
    ISBN 0–89145–977–4: $19.95
     1. Patchwork.   2. Quiltmaking. I. Title
TT835.D63   1991
746.9'7 dc20   91–43354
                                   CIP

Additional copies of this book may be ordered from:

American Quilter's Society
P.O. Box 3290
Paducah, KY 42001

@ $19.95. Add $1.00 for postage & handling.

Copyright: Carol Doak, 1992

Contents

Acknowledgments

My heartfelt thanks are extended:

To Pam Ludwig, a good friend who offered her proofreading skills when this book was in its earliest stages and who has subsequently convinced me that the word *compass* is indeed spelled with two s's.

To my dear friend Sherry Reis who asked me to go with her to a quilting class and opened my eyes to the art of quiltmaking and the joy of our deep friendship.

To my quilting students who encouraged me time and again to write this book and who made teaching the art of quiltmaking a joy.

To my good quilting friends, whose love and encouragement are very dear.

To Ginny Guaraldi for the photography used to illustrate some of the techniques.

To Victoria Faoro and her staff for their skillful expertise in making this dream a reality.

To my husband, Alan, and sons, Brian and Jeff, whose love and support allowed me the opportunity to teach quiltmaking and write this book.

Finally, to my Mom and late Dad for giving me the confidence to pursue those things in life which I found satisfying and worthwhile.

Introduction

More than a decade ago I walked into an adult education class in Worthington, Ohio, to learn "The Art of Quiltmaking." I went to the class because I had recently been transplanted from New England and the thought of making a charming quilt and new friends at the same time seemed appealing. I labored through several weeks of lessons, becoming enlightened every session about all that quilting had to offer. As interesting and fulfilling as the class was, I believe it was the all-day bus trip to a national quilt show with a local quilt guild that really "hooked" me on quilting. I walked around all day gasping for breath as I gazed at each quilt. I kept saying things like, "How can they do that with a needle?" I was just plain awestruck – and unknowingly on my way to be consumed by "The Art of Quiltmaking."

I began searching out all that I could about quilting through shows, books and classes. The search has been as rewarding as the information it has yielded.

It was not long before I was teaching that same adult education class, and subsequently many others. I have really enjoyed teaching and starting or helping others along their way. This book is the result of classes taught to both experienced quilters and new quilters and shares all of the methods and techniques I have used.

This book is written for both the new quilter and the experienced quilter. Its purpose is to start the new quilters along the way and to answer many of their questions. This book is formatted as a reference book so that as they come across a particular situation, they can readily look up the answer. For experienced quilters, it gives some new techniques to work with, some new ideas to follow and the confidence for them to please themselves. For both new and experienced quilters, I have shared many of the "Tricks of the Trade" that I have found helpful.

Quilting has been done for too long and by too many for any one person to have all the answers. What this book provides are some simplifications, approaches and methods which are used by many quilters of today, which you might find helpful in your own endeavors of this rich art.

This book is designed to give you the tools with which to create and methods with which to make your designs a reality.

Chapter One

Selecting Fabrics

Picking out fabrics is the task that is probably the most uncomfortable for new quilters and is often lamented even by the experienced. The process is difficult because it is totally against everything we know to be right. For example, if you wore a small print blouse, a striped jacket and a large print skirt out in public, you would raise more than a few eyebrows. Everyone would pity your lack of good taste. With patchwork, though, you are expected to put together such a group of fabrics and feel certain that they will work together. You already "know" in your heart that they don't "go together," so there is an instant contradiction.

You need to convince yourself that you are going to pick out *colors* much like a painter picks out his tubes of oils. The fact that some of the fabrics you select happen to be prints is not a problem. The pattern in the print will simply add texture, as do the painter's brush strokes. Now the contradiction has been eliminated.

"But why do prints work well in patchwork?" you ask. One reason is that tradition leads people to expect to see prints in patchwork. Another reason is that the small pieces which are being used are being complemented and softened by fabrics around them. It is much easier to accept a two-inch square of a large print than it is to accept a two-yard piece gathered around someone's waist.

COTTON VERSUS BLENDS

The question of whether you should use cotton fabric or blends of cotton and polyester in quilts is often asked. I don't know that one is better than the other; however, each does have certain properties which should be considered when purchasing fabric for patchwork and applique.

COTTONS have many advantages:
- 100% cotton fabric will tear along the grain line. If you are planning to tear your fabric into strips, you will want to use cotton.
- Cotton will finger press. When doing patchwork you will want to crease the fabric with your fingers along each seam you have sewn to make nice sharp angles. Cotton will do this; blends will not.
- If you plan to applique and turn the edges under with your needle (rather than basting), you will want to use cottons because of this ability to crease.
- If you plan to sew your pieces on the sewing machine, you will want the body that cotton has to offer. Blends will tend to slip and not hold those nice sharp angles.

BLENDS (fabrics which are a blend of both cotton and polyester) also offer advantages:

• Blends can be used on the backing of your patchwork. They are not difficult to quilt through.

• You can use blends in large areas such as large borders where you do not have to rely on intricate piecing. Remember, though, that you will need to cut these pieces because they will not tear well along a grain line.

Sometimes, however, the perfect fabric is available only in a blend and you may want to make concessions. Do this only with the knowledge of how your selection of fabric will affect your ability to work with it.

TYPES OF FABRICS

All set pick to out your fabrics, you walk in the door of the quilt shop and there are 500-plus bolts of fabric waiting for you to find just the right three, four or five fabrics that work nicely together. No wonder fabric selection can make one feel uncomfortable. I went into a quilt shop recently that boasted of 2,000 bolts of calicos. Even I was overwhelmed. It's time to place those fabrics into half a dozen categories. A few types of fabric will be easier to deal with than all those bolts. (See pages 195, 197, 199 and 201 for close-up photographs showing examples.)

SOLIDS are easy to describe. Any fabric which has no markings on it at all is a solid. (Figure 1-1) Solids give patchwork a contemporary look and are often used to make Amish-style quilts. Solids do, however, show any flaws in piecing (sewing together of pieces) or quilting techniques. A contrasting color quilting thread against a solid fabric will show every stitch and exactly how even and straight each is. If you are still perfecting the mechanics of patchwork and quilting, go easy with the solids or be sure to use thread that matches your fabric very closely.

MINI-PRINTS are the fabrics that have tiny, two-contrast prints. (Figure 1-2) The mini-dot fabrics would fall into this category. These fabrics look like solid colors from a distance. Your quilting designs will show up very nicely on mini-prints but the exact quilting stitch will not be very evident. You might choose more than one mini-print for your patchwork. You would probably not use mini-prints exclusively, though, because the resulting patchwork would lack excitement.

Figure 1-1

Figure 1-2

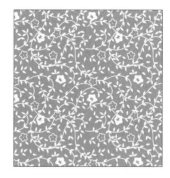

Figure 1-3

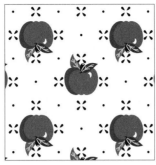

Figure 1-4

Figure 1-5

DOTS usually have a background color and then one element such as a dot, a flower, a butterfly or other figure which draws your eye as a large polka dot would. (Figure 1-3) This type of fabric adds interest; however, you probably would not want more than one dot-type fabric in your patchwork project. You will know a fabric is in this category because your eyes will have difficulty focusing on it. You will know when you are using too many "dots" because your eyes will begin to jump when looking at the fabric grouping.

CALICOS are the typical patchwork fabrics. They are small prints with one color for a background and several other colors in the print elements. (Figure 1-4) Be sure to look at this type of fabric from a distance to determine which is the predominant color. A calico fabric may have a beige background fabric with green, orange, blue and purple flowers. These may indeed be all the colors you would like to use in your quilting project; however, when you stand back from this fabric you may find that the beige is the only color visible. If you want those other colors in your quilt, you will need to select fabrics which are predominantly those colors. Some fabrics may come across with more than one color and that's fine. Just be certain to stand back at a distance to see exactly which color or colors dominate.

One advantage to using calicos is that you can suggest a color. The flower in the print might actually be red upon close examination; however, you may suggest that it is actually rust by introducing a predominantly rust fabric. From a distance, that red now looks rust. This often works well with the green and blue family as well. You may want to use more than one calico in your patchwork, depending upon how busy they are. You will know the prints are too busy to be used together if you find it difficult to focus on them both at the same time.

LARGE PRINTS are just that, fabrics with large patterns, which often have many colors. (Figure 1-5) By choosing a large print with many colors first, you can often draw from those colors, choosing other fabrics to complement.

TRICK

If you are concerned that a particular large-print fabric might make your patchwork project too busy, cut a hole out of a sheet of paper the approximate size of the patchwork piece you are planning to use and move it across the fabric to see what type of texture results. Most often, the result will be varied splashes of color.

AIRY PRINTS are large-scale prints having one background color and usually only one other contrast or color. (Figure 1-6) Airy prints can add a change of pace (by introducing a much larger scale) without adding a lot of color confusion. The large-scale prints and the airy prints both add quite a bit of interest to patchwork, but too much of a good thing can make your patchwork too busy.

STRIPES are just that, fabrics which contain stripes. Striped fabric may involve simple two-color stripes or very intricate many-colored stripes. These fabrics are exciting to work with.

The advantage of using stripes is that they lead the viewer's eye in a direction, such as around an octagon design. The mitered corners of a square or rectangle will create a framing effect. You can use different elements of the same striped fabric to add several different textures or suggestions to your patchwork. Many colored and patterned striped fabrics can suggest the entire color scheme for a quilt and then frame it as a border. (Figure 1-7)

There are many different types and scales of stripes. (Figure 1-8)

Stripes can make it look as if you actually pieced more than you did by giving the illusion of separate pieces of fabric. (Figure 1-9)

Figure 1-6

Figure 1-7

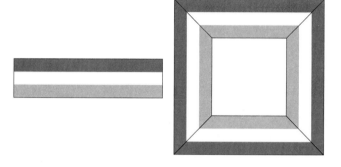

Figure 1-8

Figure 1-9

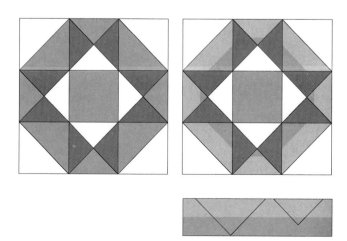

You can obtain many different looks using the same striped fabric by placing your templates on the stripes in different directions. For example, by placing the diamond in reverse directions on the stripes (below), you can achieve very attractive chevrons to fit within a block or to use as a continuous border.

Figure 1-10

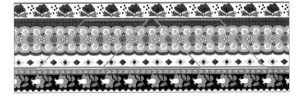

Figure 1-11

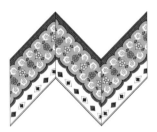

COLOR

In order to discuss color, we need to have a common understanding of the terms used. When talking about color we are referring to a number of qualities:

Hue is what we commonly mean when we say "color." There are three pure colors or hues: red, blue and yellow. There are also three secondary hues (combinations of the primary hues): green, purple and orange.

Value is used to explain whether a hue is dark or light. Adding white to a hue creates a tint. Adding black to a hue creates a shade.

Intensity is used to describe the brightness or dullness of a color.

There are many books which discuss the color wheel in great detail – the shades, the tints, the hues, the balance. Rather than attempt such a detailed explanation, I have chosen to discuss hue, value and intensity, as they relate to choosing fabrics and using them in a design. When you desire to know more, when the colors are not working and you want to know why and you are ready to delve deeper into the concepts of color, you may want to study color in greater detail by locating a book on color theory.

HUE: The colors or hues that you choose to work with will usually be those that you personally prefer. Blue is my preferred color, and most of my quilts contain some blue. It is comforting to work with colors that you prefer. Even when determined to work with a color that is not my preference, I usually manage to find a striped fabric which contains the color I am working with, along with blue. Two quilts which began as green quilts ended up being blue and green quilts because of my need to return to my preferred color. Putting blue into those green quilts was comforting and after all, those quilts were made to please me!

Sometimes the choice of color is suggested by one or more outside elements. A baby quilt for a new little girl may suggest pinks or soft feminine colors. The colors in your room decor may suggest what colors you are going to put together in a quilt. My very first quilt was made in light green (the color of the carpet chosen by the previous owner of the house), peach (the color of the drapes from our old house) and brown (the color of the furniture in the room). The need to link the colors in the bedroom was the sole motivation for putting those three colors together in a quilt.

Look around you to discover what color combinations you enjoy and copy them in your patchwork. When we first moved to New Hampshire, I was driving down the street one spring day and was treated to a very pretty blue sky against very crisp white snow, along with the deep green of the pine trees and the lighter green of the budding leaf trees. How striking those colors were together. I set out to make my next geometric wallhanging using just those colors: light blue, soft green, darker green and white. The result was a blue ribbon wallhanging called "Shades of New Hampshire." Now when those colors reveal themselves to me in nature, I know what to call them…shades of New Hampshire.

The point I am trying to make with regards to hue is that you are surrounded by colors all the time and you know what colors and color combinations are pleasing to you. You don't need the color wheel to be aware of YOUR preferences. Use these preferences when picking our your "Hues."

VALUE: Again, this is the degree of darkness or light in a color. A black and white photograph shows no hues, only values. You need value in order to have contrast and for your design to emerge. Adding white to a hue will give you tints and adding black to a hue will give you shades. In retrospect perhaps my wallhanging should have been called "Tints and Shades of New Hampshire," but a little poetic license goes a long way.

Exactly how much contrast you create in your quilt is again a matter of personal preference.

• Using fabrics that have a medium value and continue to the dark shades to create contrast will result in a "dark" quilt.

• Using fabrics that have a medium value and continue to the lightest tints will result in a very soft, light, pastel quilt.

• Using the lightest tint to the darkest shades will result in the greatest amount of contrast and will be the most graphic.

Contrast is relative and it is good to keep in mind that the lighter tints will appear larger and the darker shades will appear smaller. Knowing this, you will want to make the larger areas dark and the smaller areas light. A little bit of a light hue goes a long way. Experimenting with value during the design process by just using light and dark pencils to shade in your design will give you a sense of value before you actually introduce the color. Think of your light colors (when not used as a background) as accents. When your light colors are used as background, the relationship of the colors that you put on top will vary and will become relative. For example, a light gray on top of a white will have very little contrast, but that same gray on top of black will have great contrast. The degree of contrast is up to you. If you choose a light background and you

Figure 1-12

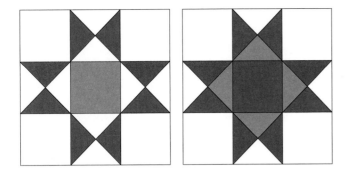

Figure 1-13

want subtle contrast, you would choose a medium fabric on top. If you choose a light background and you want great contrast, you would choose a dark shade on top. Remember, darker seems smaller, so you would probably want to increase the actual area where this great contrast is going to appear. (Figure 1-12)

This also works in reverse. A dark background with a medium fabric on top gives subtle contrast. A dark background with light fabric on top gives great contrast. Again, the lighter area will seem larger so you might want to reduce the area in size where the lighter color is being used. (Figure 1-13)

INTENSITY: This term refers to the brightness or dullness of a color. I think you could put any color together with any other color and make it work. However, intensity of a color can cause problems. Visualize a very soft baby yellow, now a true yellow and now a brilliant yellow. That is intensity.

If you were putting together a group of primary colors (the kind you associate with school box crayons: true red, true blue, true green) and then put in a soft pastel yellow, the yellow would look dull and lost. It wouldn't appear "to go" with the others. Now go back an take out that soft pastel yellow and put in a brilliant yellow. Again, the yellow now appears too strong and overpowering. All you can see is the yellow. The other colors get lost. You need a happy medium. You need that primary yellow with your primary colors for the colors "to go together." So it is not the colors themselves that have a problem, it is the relationship that they have with the colors around them.

Sometimes it is pleasing to add "just a touch" of a more intense color to spice up your patchwork. Remember, a little goes a long way and too much of a color which has greater intensity than what you are using can become "the only thing that you see." If your accent is all that your eye focuses on, you have added too much.

CATEGORIZING FABRICS

Now that you have categories in which to place your fabric, you have simplified the selection of your fabric into types with different colors. Try this exercise of looking at several different types of fabric and deciding which category they fit into. Are you looking at dots? Are you looking at a calico? Taking the time to become familiar with putting fabric into categories will make things more comfortable for you once you enter the quilt shop. As with most things in life, there are always those which are the exception and the same holds true with attempting to place ALL fabrics into categories. You will occasionally run into fabrics which are a little bit of this category and a little bit of that. Place them as best you can in relation to the other fabrics you have selected. The type of fabric which readily comes to mind would be a dot which is not large enough to create focusing problems, yet not small enough to be considered a mini-print. When this happens, place the fabric in one category or the other and when another fabric is chosen which is a classic example of one of those categories you can then decide whether you like the two fabrics together.

WHICH FIRST, THE DESIGN OR THE FABRIC?

This may sound like the familiar, "Which came first, the chicken or the egg?" question. Actually the answer to this question is a little easier – either may be first.

If you choose your fabric first, you will want to design a quilt or a block which utilizes the number of contrasts you have purchased. If you bought one dark fabric, one light fabric and two different medium fabrics, your design will need at least four different areas of contrast in order to use what you have.

If, on the other hand, you have already designed a block or quilt, you will need to determine how many different areas of contrast you would like. This will determine how many different fabrics you need to purchase. The more fabrics you use, the more intricate the design. Remember, the block can get too intricate and cause you eyes to try to focus at too much at one time. Plan carefully.

HOW MANY FABRICS ARE NEEDED?

That is another question that has no one answer. The most realistic answer is to determine how many contrasts you would like to make within your design and choose that number of contrasting fabrics. One large print and a solid fabric may be enough for your design, or you may use one dot and two mini-prints. Go with your instincts. If you feel, "that looks too busy," it probably is. I would say that three to seven different fabrics is a good range to fall within. The exception of course would be scrap quilts where any and all fabrics and colors are put together using pieces which are quite small to gain the desired effect. The other exception would be the two-fabric quilts where the contrast between just two fabrics is supported by a very graphic design.

Your needs are basic: color, contrast and variety of prints. Once you choose one fabric (a light blue dot), determine which need it fulfills and proceed to fill your other needs as indicated by what is left on your list. It is helpful in the beginning to check off the needs you have filled as you choose each fabric. It is always easier to shop if you have a shopping list.

USING A SHOPPING LIST FOR SELECTION

Having a method to fall back on will give you a feeling of confidence. While on confidence, let me stress again, please yourself. Don't make your fabric selection and then ask Uncle Harry, Aunt Em and the girl next door what they think. You will probably get three different answers because they each have their own tastes, not right, not wrong, just different.

Make out a shopping list containing the seven different categories and columns for light, medium and dark.

SHOPPING LIST			
	Light	Medium	Dark
Solid			
Mini-Prints			
Calicos			
Stripes			
Large Prints			
Airy Prints			
Dots			

I usually refer to a color by its beginning letter, B for blue, R for rust, etc. Using this method, you will be able to see right away which choices are predominantly light, medium or dark and what color is dominant.

• Begin with a color in mind – you need somewhere to begin. If you don't have any idea of color in mind, then choose your favorite color and begin there. You have the right to change your mind. Your decisions are open to discussion, so give yourself the benefit of the doubt. Perhaps you would like a group of fabric in the same color but with different values.

Figure 1-14

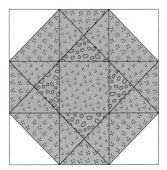 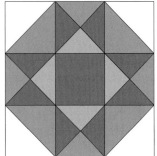

Value is the degree of darkness or lightness. Value provides you with the contrast you need in order to see a design emerge. A graphic example of a design's being lost would be the use of three different light fabrics within the same block. The fabrics may indeed be different but if they don't contrast with each other, your design will be lost. By the same token, it does not make sense to use two different fabrics which accomplish the same task. If one fabric can easily be interchanged for another and still elicit the same effect, there is no reason to use both. (Figure 1-14)

With our color in mind, go over to that color section and pick out ANY bolt which strikes your fancy. For the sake of making this example easier to understand, I will suggest that your quilt is going to be blue and rust. It makes no difference whether you begin with the blue or rust. If you are undecided, then go with your preferred color. You need to like your fabric; you will be handling it a lot. When asked once to define a "quilter," my quick answer was that a quilter is someone who buys approximately 10 yards of fabric and cuts it into upwards of 2,000 pieces and then spends months sewing those pieces back together. The moral of the story: really like the fabric you choose so you will enjoy working with it.

Once you have selected a bolt of fabric, take it away from the others and place it near a source of natural light, on its side. Stand back ten feet and contemplate.

Do you still like it? What type of fabric have you chosen? Is it a calico, solid, mini-print, stripe, dot or large and/or airy print?

Is this fabric a light fabric, a dark fabric or a medium fabric? If you started in the blue section, does the fabric you selected indeed appear to be blue from a distance?

Make the necessary notations on your shopping list and go on.

SHOPPING LIST			
	Light	Medium	Dark
Solid			
Mini-Prints			
Calicos		B	
Stripes			
Large Prints			
Airy Prints			
Dots			

• It's time to choose another fabric. Your first choice was a calico; it was blue and it was a medium shade. Your second choice will be any fabric in either the blue or rust section that is *not* a calico and is either a light fabric or a dark fabric. If you only began with one color because you didn't know what other colors to put with it, you might now want to look closely at that calico you picked out and use one of the colors in it to pick out your second fabric, perhaps a large print that is predominantly a dark rust. Take the bolt over to your first bolt and lay it on top. If you like the choice, mark your shopping list accordingly.

SHOPPING LIST			
	Light	Medium	Dark
Solid			
Mini-Prints			
Calicos		B	
Stripes			
Large Prints			R
Airy Prints			
Dots			

• It's now time to pick out your third fabric. You may choose a blue or rust fabric that is *not a calico or a large print* and is either a dark, medium or light fabric. Since you have not chosen a light fabric as of yet, this might be a good time to look for a fabric category you have not used (dot, mini-print, solid, stripe) in a lighter color. You see a very nice dot in light blue and take that bolt over and place it on top. You decide you like this with the others. Mark your shopping list.

SHOPPING LIST			
	Light	Medium	Dark
Solid			
Mini-Prints			
Calicos		B	
Stripes			
Large Prints			R
Airy Prints			
Dots	B		

Consider again the fabrics you have selected. Do you like your choices? As you place the bolts on top of each other, be willing to say, "That looks terrible!" Most of the time your reaction will be immediate, positive or negative. Go with your impulses. If you are not sure, put the bolt aside and contemplate again.

Thus far you have chosen a medium blue calico, a dark rust large print and a light blue dot fabric. They look nice together. You may continue and add mini-prints which are both light and dark or a stripe which might have both light and dark or which might have both the blue and rust in it. People are basically organized so including a few fabrics which have both of the colors you are placing together is comforting, but it is not necessary. The more fabrics you choose, the more intricate your design will be.

The more you use this exercise, the more confident you will become in picking out your fabric and it will become second nature to mentally eliminate certain categories from your shopping list. Picking out fabric can be lots of fun. The more you do it, the more you will actually enjoy it.

GENERAL SUGGESTIONS FOR FABRIC SELECTION

• One light, two medium and one dark fabric make nice combinations.

• Choose a large multicolor or calico for your first fabric and draw from its colors.

• Use a predominantly white or off-white fabric to draw the white out of your dark print fabrics. It will make your dark fabrics tend to sparkle.

• Make little bits of color appear to be your color of choice within the same shade by placing a predominantly preferred colored fabric with it. (Small amounts of red in a calico will appear to be rust if a rust is placed near the calico.)

• Brown and tans are colors which have all other colors in them. Therefore, brown shades and tints are good fabrics to go to if you need contrast but don't want to introduce a new color.

• Be aware of color combinations around you that are pleasing and copy them in your patchwork. Some sources of color combinations are found in nature, advertising, fabrics, paintings and wallpapers.

• Be aware that some fabrics are one-way prints. That means there is a definite up and down to the fabric or the image on the fabric will be upside down. This type of fabric requires special placement and if you are a beginner it might be wise to initially avoid these fabrics. It is just one more thing you would need to consider. As you become more experienced and have less to consider, these fabrics will be fine to include. You may on the other hand want to use a one-way print and not pay attention to the direction of the images. That is your choice also.

WHEN CHOOSING FABRIC ALWAYS:

- *Take the bolt away from the others.*

It is necessary to take the fabric away from the other fabrics which surround it. Looking at the fabric surrounded by other bolts can suggest colors which do not exist. You need to see the fabric alone first.

- *Lay the bolt on its side so you are only looking at the edge.*

Your perception of how a fabric will work in small pieces is easier to imagine if you indeed are only looking at a small section at a time. Sometimes you may even want to cup your hands in the shape of a triangle and place it over sections of large print fabrics to gain a perspective of how the large print will work up in patchwork. By the same token, it is often helpful to fold the fabric back to reveal different sections of striped material to gain a perspective on how it will appear in patchwork.

- *Stand ten feet back from the bolt and look at it.*

Close examination of fabric is not a realistic way to make choices. It is often the quickest way to be assured of disappointment. To see exactly which color dominates, you really need to get far enough away.

- *Look at the fabric in good natural light.*

Colors and fabrics take on different looks in different lights. Ideally you should place your fabric near a natural light but not in it. Don't place your fabric in front of an open window and then look into the window. You need to have the light at your back. Placing the fabric near the window, with the window to your back, is ideal.

DECIDING HOW TO USE THE FABRICS IN YOUR DESIGN

You have a group of fabrics in front of you and you also have a drawing of patchwork design. How do you decide what color or fabric to put where?

There are three methods you might like to try in order to visualize your block design in fabric. Remember, if you shaded your design in and your darkest color is in the center, choose your darkest fabric for that area.

- Choose one of your fabrics as a background color; lay it out in front of you in approximately the size your block will be. Then take your other fabrics and lay them on top and next to each other to get a rough idea of how each fabric looks next to the others. Move the fabrics around until you find a combination you like.

- Use colored pencils to color your design in the approximate colors of your fabric. Be sure to try to approximate the degree of color whether light, medium or dark. It also helps to approximate the type of fabric, adding stripes and dots, etc. where they are going to be used.

- Make a fabric mock-up to scale by cutting small pieces of the fabrics you think you might like to use and pasting them right on your graph paper. This last method is the most time-consuming method, but gives the truest picture.

All three of these methods give you a good picture of how your block design will come across in patchwork.

TRICK

If you have finished blocks and are trying to decide their placement in a quilt such as in a sampler quilt, try looking through the view finder of a camera or the large end of a pair of binoculars. The blocks will be seen at a distance so you will have a better sense of the finished quilt.

Chapter Two

Yardage

Once the fabrics have been selected, the next question is, "How much do I need to buy?" Most new quilters go on a mad rampage of buying ¼ yard pieces of many fabrics and begin a collection of scraps with little or no purpose. Having lots of scraps is not necessarily a bad thing; however, a few guidelines are always helpful.

I was once asked during a lecture how much yardage I purchase when I am buying a fabric just to have it on hand. My immediate response was, "All of it!" But seriously, like most quilters, I love fabric but have limited resources. I need to be somewhat realistic when deciding how much to purchase. There are basically two ways to buy fabrics:

• You have a particular project in mind and you now need to buy fabric to make it.

• You have no project in mind, but you have found a particular fabric or group of fabrics that you feel the need to purchase today because the fabric will be perfect for a project someday. Perhaps it is even on sale today, so you can increase your supply relatively inexpensively.

Both of these methods are acceptable for the quilter. We'll take a look at guidelines for each in this chapter.

SOME FABRIC BASICS

Most of the cotton and cotton-blend fabric that you purchase to use for quilting will be sold from a bolt and be approximately 44" to 45" wide from selvage to selvage. For the purposes of estimating yardage needs, I always use 40" as the fabric width. This allows for shrinkage and extra-wide selvages – and 40 is an easier number to work with in calculations. Fabric is purchased by the yard and portions of the yard. Unless I need to be very precise with my inches, I use the following figures:

1 yard	= 36"	(36" x 40")
¾ yard	= 27"	(27" x 40")
½ yard	= 18"	(18" x 40")
¼ yard	= 9"	(9" x 40")
⅛ yard	= 4.5"	(4.5" x 40")

ESTIMATING YARDAGE

Often you may have a particular project in mind when you select and purchase fabrics, so you will want to know how to estimate the yardage required.

Sometimes you will easily have a sense of the amount needed. If you are making a 15" pillow using three different fabrics, a ¼-yard (9" x 40") piece would be plenty for the patchwork. I hardly ever purchase just ⅛ yard because 4.5" is such a limiting size to work with and might be smaller than one side of the patch I need to cut. The extra ⅛ yard will not be wasted.

But, there are other questions you need to ask before purchasing your yardage, even in seemingly simple situations. Do you want to use one of the fabrics for the back of the 15" pillow? If so, you had better buy another ½ yard (18" x 40").

Is your pillow going to have a ruffle around it? If so, figure the yardage needed. Multiply the width of the ruffle by two for the width of the strip needed (it will be folded in half) and allow enough length for the strip to go around the pillow one and a half to two times. Therefore, a 3" ruffle to go around the 15" square pillow needs to be about 6" wide and 120" long. To make the length needed, it is acceptable to piece strips cut across the width of the yardage. If you can cut about 40 inches of strip from selvage to selvage, you will need to make three cuts each 6" wide, which means a total of 18 inches of fabric will be used. You will therefore need another half yard of fabric for your ruffle. This ½-yard measurement does not allow for seam allowance, shrinkage or straightening of the edge of your fabric. This means you will want a little more than a ½-yard piece.

Basically, I look at each place I am going to use this particular fabric and estimate how much yardage I will need to cut out that portion of the project.

BE GENEROUS IN YOUR ESTIMATES: When sewing clothing, you look on the back of the pattern, choose your view and buy the exact prescribed amount of fabric. Quiltmaking is different. You must determine the amount needed yourself and allow for some variation. I tend to be generous in my estimates because:

• Fabric cut from the bolt is seldom cut along the grain line, so you will need to straighten it. A few inches may be lost in this process.

• All fabric must first be prewashed; washing and drying often results in shrinkage.

• You may change your mind and want to use more of a particular fabric.

• It's easy to forget to add ½" for seam allowances (¼" for each side) when you're calculating.

For these reasons I always figure my yardage exactly or approximately and then add a ¼ yard.

In dressmaking any leftover fabric usually becomes a white elephant because you certainly would not have enough to make another dress. With quilting, even the smallest amount of fabric left over will probably end up in a future project and will evoke many memories.

FURTHER GUIDELINES: Be sure to buy enough fabric to cut your largest piece. For example, if you are making a quilt that is going to be 90" long and the last one-piece border is 8" wide, you should buy three yards of fabric – a piece that is 108" long. If you need four pieces that are 8½" wide by 90½" long you will be able to cut these out of a three-yard piece. Four times the 8½" is 34" which would leave you about 6" by 108" left over for piecing. As I mentioned before, I always consider all fabric width as 40" to allow for a little leeway.

Always plan on cutting your borders or lattice a little larger than the exact measurement to allow for your quilt to grow. When working with several hundred pieces of fabric, in spite of your best intentions your quilt may become larger than it was supposed to be. Fabric may allow a little bit of easing, but if you need to allow your quilt to be even a little larger, the borders or lattice that you have already cut larger will accommodate the new dimensions. I call this my insurance policy. If all else fails, the quilt is made larger than intended.

Approximate the total yardage of the project and be sure to buy enough fabric to fill that yardage. A general rule of thumb is that a full-size quilt top takes approximately 10 yards and a queen-size, 12 yards.

If you are making a sampler, cut your large pieces for borders, etc. first and put them aside. Use what is left over to make your patchwork blocks. Remember that you would not want to buy 10 one-yard pieces for the full-size quilt if you have planned on one piece of fabric for a border. You need to buy a long enough piece of yardage for your largest piece.

A SHORTAGE CAN BE AN OPPORTUNITY: I don't agonize over exact yardage requirements. Should I run out of a particular fabric that I've intended to use, I don't panic. I accept the situation and come up with an alternative. If you look at this situation as positive and not negative, you will never agonize over figuring yardages because you will not fear the possibility of running out. When you run out of a fabric, you are forced to be creative, to come up with an alternative. Do you have any idea how many wonderful creative ideas have evolved from poor planning? Enjoy these situations – don't fear them. Your successes in getting around these setbacks will give you the confidence to go on. I can almost guarantee that the creativity you use when you run out of fabric will probably be what sets your quilt apart from the norm.

FIGURING EXACT YARDAGE

There will be times when you want to determine the exact yardage a project will require. There are several methods for doing that.

USING A FORMULA: I use a formula to figure how much fabric is needed for a project when I know the number and size of the pieces required.

YARDAGE FORMULA

Number of pieces needed times the width of the piece in inches = *A*

A divided by 40 = Number of rows of pieces needed (round off to next highest number if necessary)

Number of rows times the height of the piece in inches = the number of inches needed down the selvage.

For example, if you have a shape that is being repeated many times in a particular quilt, count the total number of pieces needed. If you are making 12 blocks each containing four (3" x 5") rectangles of the same fabric:

1.   You would add ½" for seam allowance (¼" each side), which means you'll need a 3½" x 5½" rectangle.

2.   Twelve patchwork blocks times 4 rectangles means you will need 48 (3½" x 5½") rectangles.

3.   48 times 3½" equals 168 running inches (*A*).

4.   (*A*) 168 divided by 40 = 4.2 rows or 5 rows.

5.   Five rows times the height of 5½" equals 27½" of fabric needed.

If dealing with numbers is not your cup of tea, you are not alone. Sensing many a frustrated quilter, several authors have published books with nothing but charts to tell you how much fabric you need to purchase in order to make a certain number of units of a particular shape. Acquire one of these books, familiarize yourself with the tables and how to use them, and you will never regret your purchase.

TRICK

WHEN YOU RUN OUT OF FABRIC

Problem: You intended to use a length of fabric for a border, but you don't have enough without putting in a seam. If you just seam the fabric, you have announced to all, "I didn't have enough fabric so I had to seam it."

Solution: What you can do is piece a design in the center, between thirds or in the corners which will look intentional. These pieces will draw your eye to what would have been problem, making it an area of interest.

Problem: You have run out of a particular fabric in your piecing of several of the same blocks.

Solution: Introduce a new shade, which will add more interest to your block and then place these new and interesting blocks in balanced locations. As long as your use of fabric is balanced it will not look awkward.

The idea is to look for answers to problems as they arise and turn your lemons into refreshing lemonade.

USING GRAPH PAPER: For the visually oriented quilter, graph paper can be used to determine yardage required. Make each square across the top of your graph paper equal to an inch and count out 40. Draw a line across the top edge of the 40 squares to indicate the full fabric width and use the area beneath this for estimating. Reserve space for various pieces which need to be cut and shade in the areas as they are used up. This method will give you a plan for cutting the needed shapes from the fabric. As you shade in the areas to be used, you will see exactly what leftover fabric will be available. How much yardage you need can be easily determined by counting the squares down the side. (Figure 2-1)

PURCHASING YARDAGE WITH NO PROJECT IN MIND

• The general rule I follow when buying fabric to have on hand is to purchase a three-yard piece if it is a calico, solid, stripe, mini-print, dot or conservative large print. Having a three-yard piece allows me to use this fabric for my biggest piece in a queen-size coverlet.

• If the fabric is particularly bold and I know I would never use it as a full border but only want to use it for piecing, I buy a one-yard piece. One yard will allow me to use it often in the piecing of a full-size quilt.

If you have fabric on hand, you may take one or two pieces and go off to buy some others to complete a project. It's helpful to have fabrics on hand. Fabric is your means of creating color and texture so you need to have a supply in order to create. You will find that most quilters have quite a love affair with their fabrics. The fabrics, after all, are what inspire and enable quilters to make their ideas realities.

Figure 2-1

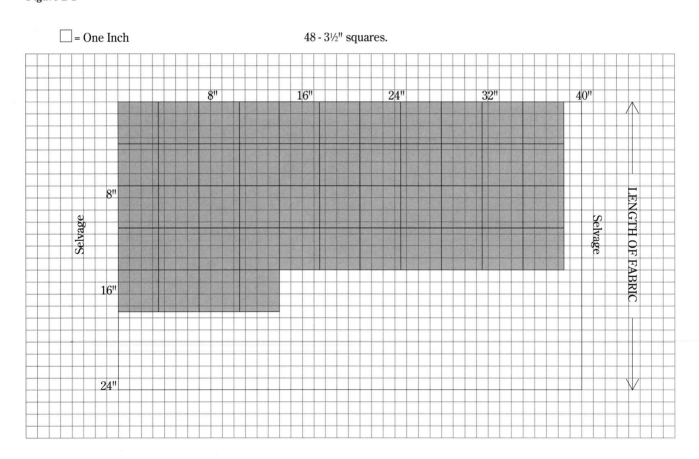

☐ = One Inch   48 - 3½" squares.

PREPARING FABRICS

Once you have purchased your fabrics, you will need to decide whether or not to prewash them. In the past, all the cotton fabrics used in quilting were generally prewashed in order to preshrink the fabric and insure that the darker fabrics would not run or bleed once they were used in a quilt. Another reason for prewashing was to remove the sizing in the fabric so the process of hand quilting was a little easier.

Today, that general rule is still followed by most who hand piece, hand applique and hand quilt. Those who machine piece and machine quilt often do not prewash their fabrics in order to take advantage of the stiffness of the unwashed fabric. Also, shrinkage after construction makes the fabric seem to "pucker" around the machine quilting.

PREWASHING FABRICS: I prewash my cotton fabrics for quilting. My general rule of thumb is to wash all the light fabrics together in warm water in the washing machine and tumble them in the dryer until they are almost dry. I then take them out and quickly iron them with a dry iron while they are still damp. When ironing, I try to run the iron only down the length of the fabric so the fabric is not stretched out of shape. I have been washing cotton fabrics for 10 years and only recently realized how much easier it is to use the squared end of the ironing board for this purpose.

The product that I have been using exclusively for washing all my cotton fabrics is called Orvus® paste. It is actually a horse soap and can be purchased from your local tack shop or feed and grain store. This product is a gentle soap which will not pull the dyes out of fabric as readily as one of the harsher detergents, and it rinses out easily. I use three tablespoons to a quarter of a cup in a washing machine load of warm water. The amount needed will vary depending upon how hard or soft your water is.

You will want to make sure the darker fabrics that you are using in your quilt will not run even after they have been washed. You can wash these separately and check the rinse water for any color change, or you can snip a piece of fabric and test it by allowing it to dry on a white paper towel to see if it bleeds. Remember, though, that a dark fabric which did not run when you used Orvus® may run if a harsher detergent is used once it is part of a quilt. If a darker fabric continues to run and you still want to use it in a quilt, be sure to test it against the lightest fabric you are using in the quilt to see if the lighter fabric will be affected. You can do this by allowing a wet piece of the darker fabric to dry on top of a wet piece of your lightest fabric.

NOT PREWASHING FABRICS: The sizing in unwashed fabric makes the fabric stiff, which can be a help when you are using the rotary cutter, sewing through the machine and then allowing the fabric to pucker up around the machine quilting once the quilt is washed. For these reasons, many "machine workers" like to wash fabrics after the project is quilted. This is not a problem; however, you do need to take care that the fabric you are going to use will not run in the finished project the first time it is washed. You will want to pretest your fabric by snipping pieces of your suspect fabrics, soaking them in warm water and Orvus®, and letting them dry against each other on a paper towel. Check the water, the lighter fabrics, and the paper towel for any bleeding. The same theory holds true here – as long as your lightest fabric is not affected by the bleeding, you can be fairly confident that you can go ahead and use the fabric and wash it after it has been made into a project. If you are washing after the project is completed, be sure to allow for the fact that your project is going to shrink in overall size.

Chapter Three

The Grid System

Figure 3-1

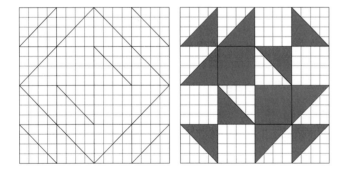

The majority of traditional patchwork blocks are based upon a square that has been divided into a number of equal sections. Many times designers begin with a grid, which enables them to more easily develop designs appropriate for patchwork.

Sometimes the grid used will be very apparent in the finished block, but other times it will not. Each line in the grid does not have to be used as a part of the final design. The grid is simply a guide. The designer has the option of using or not using each of the grid's lines. For example the block design in Figure 3-1 uses only some of the lines in the grid. Lines can be added diagonally between intersections of the grid and sections of the grid can be evenly divided by additional lines without changing the type of grid. In Figure 3-2, both designed blocks remain based on the grid at the top, even though the grid is used very differently in each and results in blocks with varying divisions.

COMMON BLOCK GRIDS

Later on in the chapter we will look at how to determine the grid used, and how to use grids in designing. But, first, let's take a look at a few traditional blocks designed using some of the most common grids.

On the following pages are examples of four-patch, nine-patch, five-patch, and seven-patch blocks.

THE FOUR PATCH: A square which has been divided in half, quarters or eighths across the top and down the sides is a four patch. Even if diagonal lines are added, as in Figure 3-2, the block is still a four patch. The traditional blocks shown on page 28 are all four-patch patterns.

THE NINE PATCH: A square which has been divided in thirds or sixths across the top and down the sides is a nine patch. Again, added lines such as those in Figure 3-3 do not change the grid type. The traditional blocks shown on page 29 are all nine-patch patterns.

Figure 3-2

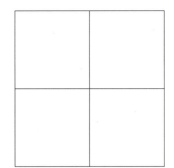

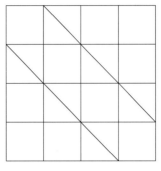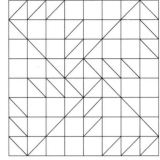

Figure 3-3

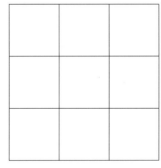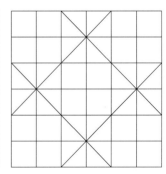

The Four Patch

Dotted lines indicate the original grid format.

Yankee Puzzle

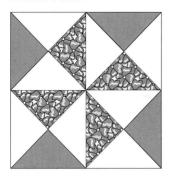

Clay's Choice

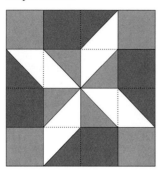

Windmill

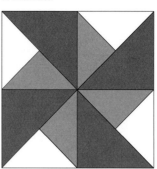

Windblown Square

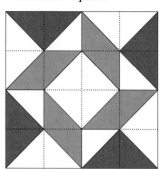

Dutchman's Puzzle

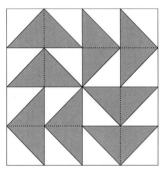

Sawtooth Star

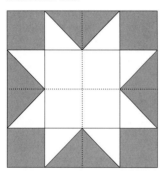

Road To Oklahoma

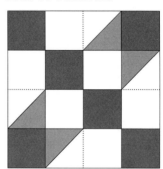

Ribbon Star

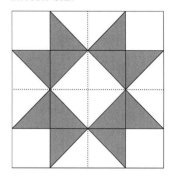

Broken Dishes or Birds in Air

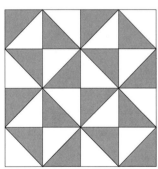

Columns

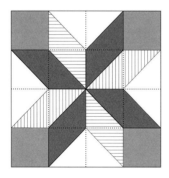

Bread Basket (*applique handle*)

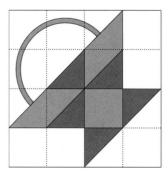

Sawtooth and Star

Northumberland Star

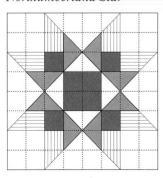

The Square Deal

Unknown

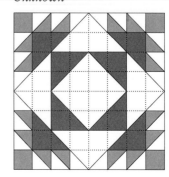

Square and Star

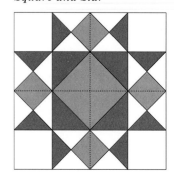

The Nine Patch

Dotted lines indicate the original grid format.

Shoofly

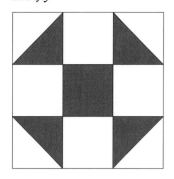

Ohio Star or Variable Star

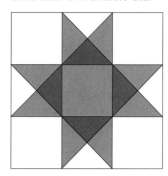

54-40 or Fight

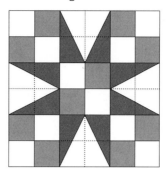

Double Nine Patch

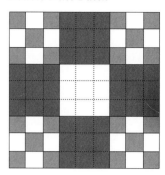

Union Squares

Friendship Star

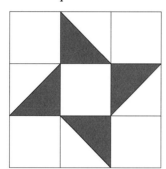

Weathervane

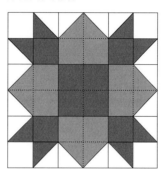

Turkey Tracks

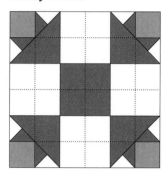

Winged Square

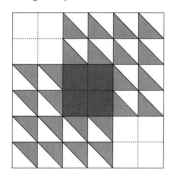

Steps To The Altar

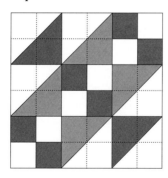

Sherman's March

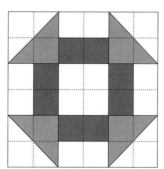

Rolling Stones

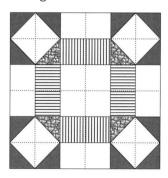

Sage Bud

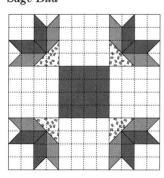

King David's Crown

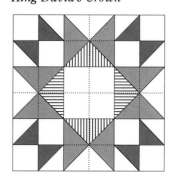

Dolly Madison's Star

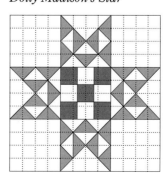

Pine Tree

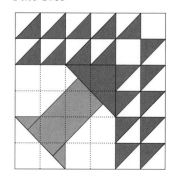

Figure 3-4

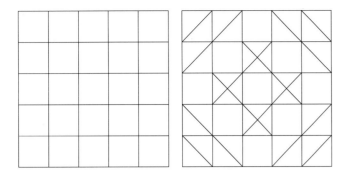

THE FIVE PATCH: A square that has been divided into fifths or tenths across the top and down the sides is a five patch. Again, lines added in a diagonal fashion or evenly between the fifths, as in Figure 3-4, do not change this grid. Some traditional five-patch patterns are shown on page 31.

THE SEVEN PATCH : A square which has been divided into seven sections across the top and down the sides is a seven patch. The design drawn may include diagonal lines as well, as in Figure 3-5. Some traditional seven-patch patterns are shown on page 32.

EXCEPTIONS TO THE RULE: As with most things in life, there are always a few exceptions. In the case of patchwork grids, sometimes a block has been divided in a particular grid and then one or more of the units inside the block is further divided in a different grid. An example of such an exception is the Double Nine Patch Block. The block is divided into thirds, but then some of the thirds are then divided into *thirds* again, rather than in half. Another example of such an exception is the five-patch block called New Mexico. The block is divided into fifths, but then some of the one-fifth sections are divided into thirds, rather than in half.

Figure 3-5

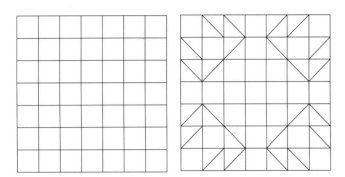

The Five Patch

Dotted lines indicate the original grid format.

The Wedding Ring

Jack-in-the-Box

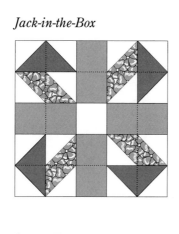

Farmer's Daughter

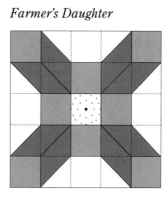

Queen Charlotte's Crown

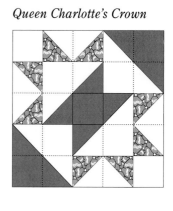

Cake Stand

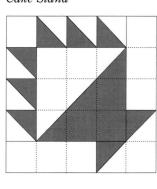

Stamp Basket (includes applique)

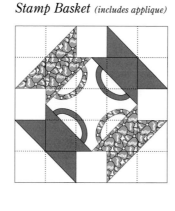

Mexican Star

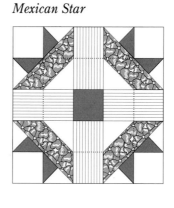

Crazy Ann

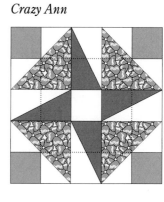

Unknown

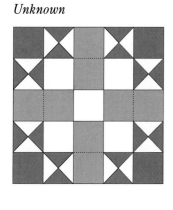

Four X Star

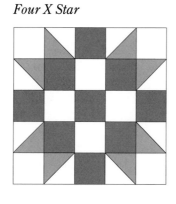

Handy Andy

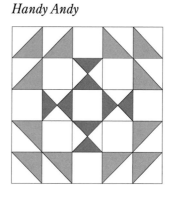

Sister's Choice

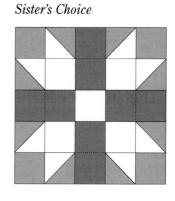

Providence

King David's Crown

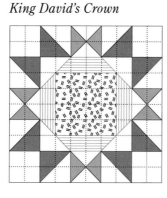

New Mexico

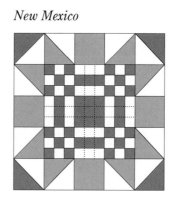

Odd Fellow's Patch

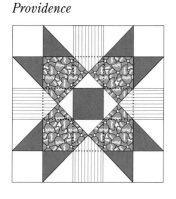

The Seven Patch

Dotted lines indicate the original grid format.

Bear's Paw

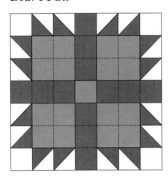

Autumn Leaf *(applique stems)*

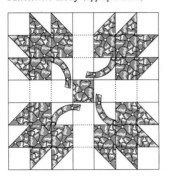

Basket *(applique handle)*

Tree of Paradise

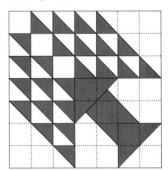

Rosebud

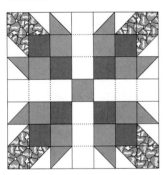

Dove in the Window

The Question Block

Lincoln's Platform

Prickly Pear

Country Roads

Cluster of Lilies

David and Goliath

Cross and Crown

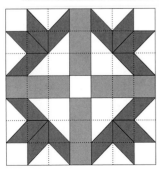

Autumn Tints

Our Country

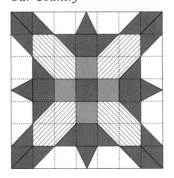

Feather Star

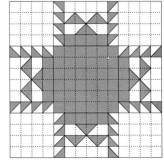

WHY GRIDS ARE IMPORTANT

These types of divisions across blocks are your basic grid system. Why do you want to know this? Because this is the system that is going to allow you to do the following two things: redraw a block and create a new block design.

The first is to enable you to copy patchwork blocks. If you can determine what grid a particular block was drawn on, then you can reproduce that block by drawing up that grid and connecting the lines in the same manner. Some blocks are more obvious than others.

DETERMINING THE GRID USED

I use one of two methods to determine what type of grid was used. The first method which will work quite often is to search out a standard size square within the block which repeats itself across the block and count the number across. You can count vertically or horizontally across it, and may need to occasionally jump up or down in the block to find the next square. You may also sometimes need to count as a square two or four triangles which fit together to make the square. See the examples in Figure 3-6.

If the design does not lend itself to that method, then I grab my trusty plastic sewing ruler which has ⅛-grid line on it and place it over the square to see how the design fits into a grid set over it. This method works well when you see a photograph or small drawing of a block that you would like to copy. (Figure 3-7)

COPYING BLOCKS USING A GRID

First, determine the grid so you can draw up the same grid in whatever size you would like.

Secondly, you begin with row one and column one and make any lines necessary to copy the design. Continue down row one and then on to each successive row. As you become more and more familiar with patchwork, you will find that you no longer are copying the design square by square but more section by section, as shown in Figure 3-8.

With this method, as long as you can determine how many equal divisions are made in a patchwork block, you can reproduce any block. The more you do it, the better you will become at reproducing blocks.

Figure 3-6

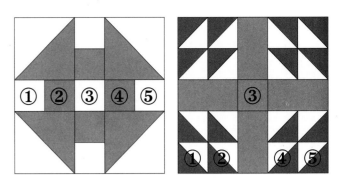

Figure 3-7

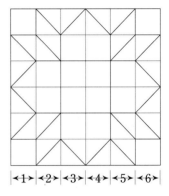

<1> <2> <3> <4> <5> <6>

Figure 3-8

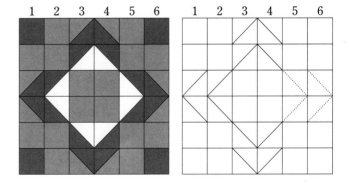

Figure 3-9

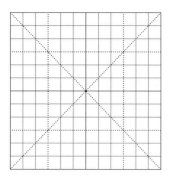

Figure 3-10

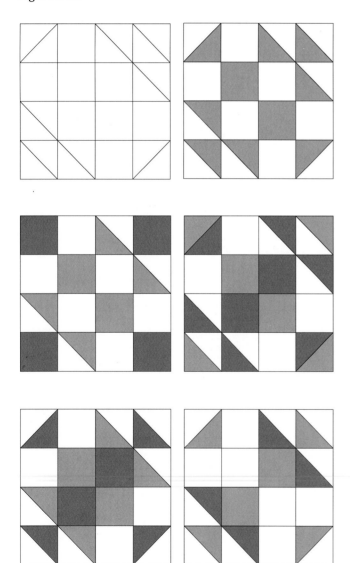

DESIGNING BLOCKS USING A GRID

The second thing the grid system is going to enable you to do is to design your own blocks. If you draw a grid up and start to make lines and shade in areas, you will start to see designs develop – many, many designs.

For the sake of example, we will consider that we would like to design a 12" block based upon a four patch. It is not necessary for you to draw blocks full size for the purpose of design: that won't be necessary until we need full-size templates (pattern pieces). For instance, if you are using ¼" graph paper, drawing a 3" square on the graph paper with 12 squares would be a 12" block drawn to scale (¼" = 1"). (Figure 3-9)

Divide the block in half, vertically and horizontally. You have just made your first division for a four patch. You may continue to divide those sections in half again, horizontally or vertically. As you see a design start to develop, shade areas in with colored pencils. Once you have drawn a design you would like to make into fabric, draw it up again full scale (as a 12" square) so you may make template pieces.

This method of drawing a blank grid and filling it in randomly with lines until a design begins to emerge is the only way I know to create. That blank piece of graph paper is probably your most creative tool. Very often, leaving a piece of graph paper by the telephone for random doodles can lead to many wonderful designs. You can take one grid block and make several copies of it and come up with many different overall designs by dissecting it differently. Shading in another way can lead to whole new avenues and entirely different designs. (Figure 3-10.)

This same concept will work for each of the basic grids. Bear in mind that the more divisions made in the block, the greater the number of pieces to be sewn together.

COMMON PATCHWORK SHAPES: You will soon notice that certain shapes develop over and over again in order to make many of the designs. The more common shapes are the following:

- The square. (Figure 3-11)
- The right angle isosceles triangle (two equal sides and one right angle). (Figure 3-12)
- The equilateral triangle (all sides equal). (Figure 3-13)
- The rhomboid (which can actually be two triangles put together). (Figure 3-14)
- The rectangle (opposite sides equal and four right angles). (Figure 3-15)
- Triangle sets (combining an isosceles – two equal sides – with two right scalene triangles – no sides equal – to form a square). (Figure 3-16)

Most often you will see these shapes used together to make designs. Examples are shown in Figure 3-17 and 3-18.

Figure 3-17

Ohio Star
(squares and triangles)

Figure 3-18

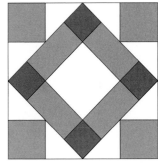

Ring Around The Posey
(squares, triangles and rectangles)

COMMON PATCHWORK SHAPES

Figure 3-11: Square

Figure 3-12: Right Angle Isosceles Triangle

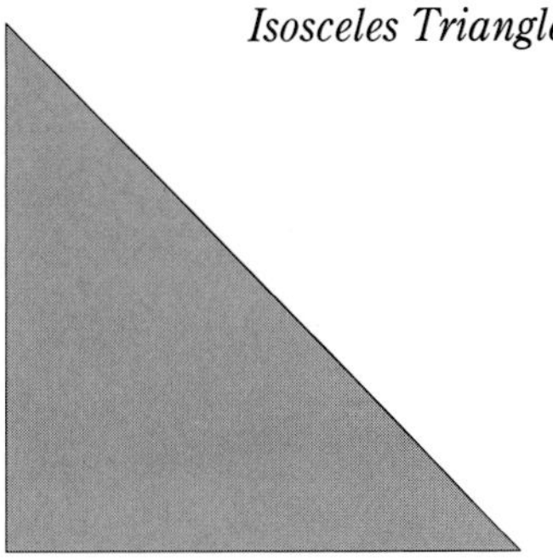

Figure 3-13: Equilateral Triangle

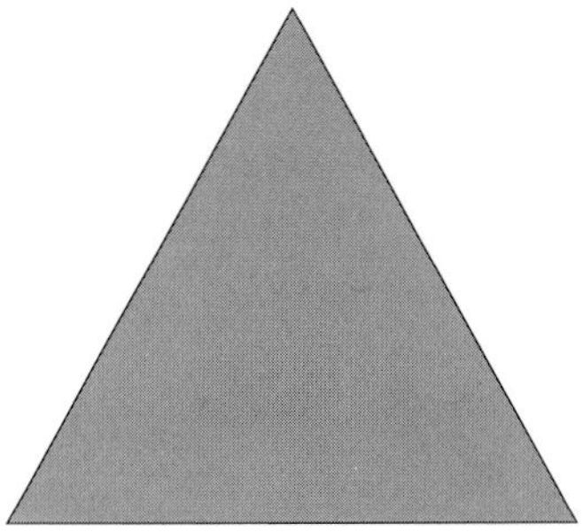

Figure 3-14: Rhomboid

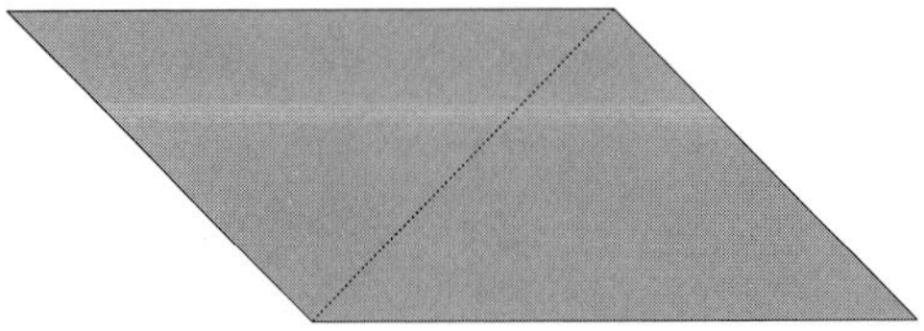

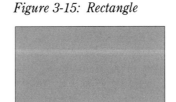

Figure 3-15: Rectangle

Figure 3-16: Triangle Set

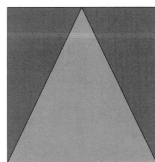

Figure 3-19

Figure 3-20

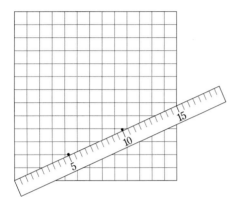

Figure 3-21

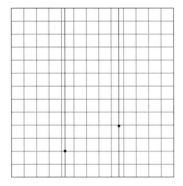

Figure 3-22

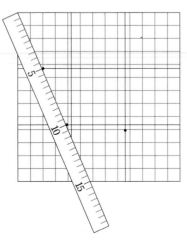

DIVIDING YOUR BLOCKS: Working with blocks that are easily divided into inches makes your task a bit easier. An even number of inches is easily divided equally into a four patch. A block size that is evenly divided into thirds (3, 9, 12, 15 etc.) easily makes a simple 9 patch. A block size that is evenly divided by fifths (5, 10, 15, 20) easily makes a simple five patch. Finally a block size evenly divided by sevenths (7, 14, 21, 28 etc.) easily makes a simple seven patch.

DIVIDING ANY SIZE BLOCK EVENLY: What should you do if the block size that you want to make does not easily divide into your grid? For example, you want to make a 13" 9-patch block. The following trick will be an invaluable tool.

• Draw a 13" block on graph paper. (Figure 3-19)

• Take a ruler and mark with chalk the next highest number above 13 which is easily divisible by 3. In this case that number would be 15.

• Divide the ruler into thirds with the chalk up to 15. You would make a chalk mark at the 5" and 10" intervals.

• Place the beginning of the ruler at the point where the bottom left hand corner is and slide the ruler up diagonally along the right vertical line until it meets the 15" mark. Place a dot with your pencil on the graph paper where the 5" and 10" intervals fall. These points may or may not fall on a line of your graph paper. (Figure 3-20)

• Using your ruler, draw a vertical line from top to bottom at each of those two points, being sure to hold your ruler parallel to your graph lines. (Figure 3-21)

• Repeat the last two steps, beginning at either adjoining corner to obtain the divisions across the other side of the block. (Figure 3-22)

Some examples:

• A 15" 7-patch block – The next number that you can divide evenly by seven which is higher than 15 is 21" on the ruler. Divide 21 into sevenths with division marks at the 3, 6, 9, 12, 15, 18, 21 points.

• A 10" 9 patch – The next number that you can divide evenly by three which is higher than 10 is 12" on the ruler. Divide 12 into thirds with division marks at the 4, 8 & 12 points.

• A 12" 5 patch – The next number that you can divide evenly by 5 which is higher than 12 is 15" on the ruler. Divide 15 into fifths with division marks at the 3, 6, 9, 12, 15 points.

What you are actually doing is dividing your ruler as if it were the perfect block size for that grid and then placing it diagonally on your imperfect block size.

It may happen at some time that the number that it is necessary for you to go to will be so high that it will be necessary for you to go off the block in order to make your divisions. In this case just extend the side line of your block so it will intersect with the ruler. Even if your last few divisions are not made inside your block, the line drawn down through your block will still divide it equally.

This tool allows you to make any size block in any size grid, placing no limitations on your design. An example of a 15" 7-patch block is shown in Figure 3-23.

When you have used this tool a few times it will become second nature. It affords you complete control and is well worth learning. It will give you the ability to copy or design any grid block in any size.

THE FOUR ELEMENTS OF PATCHWORK

Patchwork has four different elements which come together to create the whole block:
- Graph paper design with values (lights and darks)
- Color
- Fabric texture (category)– dots, mini-prints, stripes, etc.
- Quilting designs

You have just begun with graph paper so it is not necessary to create all the interest or detail of the design at this point. Once you have developed your design on graph paper, you will want to use values (darks and lights) or colors to gain some perspective of how it is going to look. You can shade areas with a regular pencil in varying degrees of dark, medium and light to gain a perspective of the design.

I always send students home from their first basic quilting class with the assignment of designing their own nine patch. Many leave with a look of fear on their faces, but they always come back with a sense of confidence. By drawing up their grid and just jumping in to connect lines and shade in basic shapes, they see patterns develop and they begin to determine things that they like and things that they don't. One design follows another, until their favorites arrive back at class. By doing this exercise, you gain a real understanding of not only the blocks you have created, but also of many blocks that others have drawn.

Figure 3-23

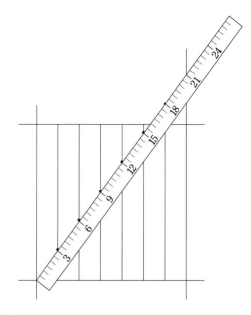

Figure 3-24

Bear Paw

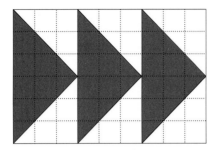

Flying Geese

Figure 3-25

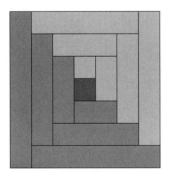

Log Cabin

NAMING BLOCKS

Now it may be that you have designed a block that you will see worked up in fabric or published, with one or more names attributed to it. The multiple names have probably resulted because several people thought it was a new block and they each gave it a different name. Different areas of the country gave a different name to the same block. The names given to blocks are helpful as a source of reference and as a source of theme or sentiment. When you design a block, give it a name if for no other reason than to be able to refer to that specific design. You may want to name your block in order to create a bit of symbolism in your patchwork. The geometric shapes are sometimes used as representative of other objects. (Figure 3-24)

Very often, sentiment is involved as well in the design and naming of a block such as with the Log Cabin block. The first time I heard that name used about a quilt block, I still remember that puzzled feeling I felt when I could no way see any house. The name Log Cabin is primarily symbolic. (Figure 3-25)

The center square is supposed to be the chimney or the hearth when done in the red shades and represents the warmth in the home. When the center block is done in yellow it is a window and represents a light in the window and hospitality. All of this from the color of the center square? The strips going around the outside represent the logs and are often referred to as logs. One side of the block is traditionally light to signify the good in life and the other side dark, to signify the bad. When this block is being sewn it sometimes is referred to as "building" another log cabin block.

Some blocks have been given very simple names when perhaps nothing else seemed right. If it is your block, you can give it any name you would like.

Chapter Four

Graph Paper

GRAPH PAPER –
MY TICKET TO DESIGN

If I had to save the tools that I use in quilting from certain destruction, my graph paper would probably be at the head of the list. Without it, I wouldn't have the ability to create intricate and interesting designs. I would soon lose interest in randomly sewing one shape to another. I need the graph paper to draw up my blocks. Graph paper allows me to draw straight lines that intersect with others correctly. I need the graph paper to draw blocks and quilts to scale. I need the graph paper to get some sort of a perspective on the design, whether it be for a block, a wallhanging or an entire quilt. I don't really get the whole picture, but I do get the graphics of how the design will interact.

Contrary to popular belief, the majority of designs are not conceived and then drawn. The majority of designs are a series of positive and negative decisions. A line is drawn and you either agree or disagree with the effect it has created. That is why it is so important to please yourself. You can't try to decide what others will or will not like. Usually, as the design begins to emerge, the excitement builds and you begin to lose yourself in the design process. It is that excitement that gives you the motivation to go on and select the fabric, sew it together and then finally quilt it to see your design become a reality. My personal feeling is that it was that excitement of design that motivated earlier quilters to give their blocks names, some of

which are very symbolic. Their design was important to them and they felt it warranted its own name.

Graph paper allows me to be creative, to experiment, to jump in and try something without investing hours of sewing. It gives me a plan to follow, a step-by-step visual instruction manual. It allows me to ponder the best way to make templates. It also allows me to change my mind if a better idea comes to light. When I want to relax and "play" at quilting, it allows me a fresh new sheet to try something new, to search for new possibilities or to put down on paper ideas in my head or even to begin ideas which were not in my head. Creativity is not a preplanned design, but rather a series of decisions that are made along the way to making a design. Graph paper is my beginning.

It comes in various size sheets and pads and in various size grids. The most convenient paper to use for full size blocks is an 18" x 21" pad of ¼" grid. Most of your blocks will be smaller than 21", so this size will accommodate the full size blocks that you would want to draw. The small pads of 8½" x 11" graph paper are fine for working blocks out to scale and drawing 8" or smaller full-size blocks. The larger pads of smaller grids (6, 8 and even 10 squares to the inch) are nice for working large quilts out to scale.

Figure 4-1

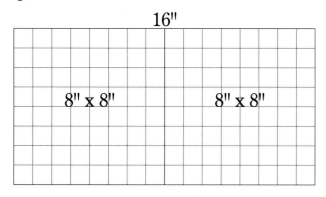

16"

8" x 8"   8" x 8"

Figure 4-2

 = 3"

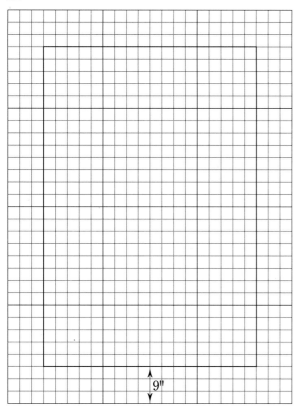

9"

DESIGNING QUILTS TO SCALE

Thus far, graph paper has been used to design your blocks based upon the grid system. But there are many other uses. Not only can you design your blocks to scale, but you can also design entire wallhangings and large quilts to scale on your graph paper.

First, take a large sheet of graph paper and assign a scale. For instance, you can make each small square equal to an inch as long as your paper has enough squares on it to accommodate the number of inches you are making. If not, make each square equal to 2" and work your quilt out on that size scale. My personal preference is to use the pads with 8 squares to an inch with the 1" intervals denoted with a heavier line. This type of graph paper allows me to count the bigger one inch square units knowing that each contains 8" to the scale. Therefore, ten 1" blocks would equal 80" to scale. The example in Figure 4-1 shows two 8" blocks which total 16" drawn to scale.

Second, draw your limitations. If you are drawing a quilt, you will want to draw the outside edges. You also will want to draw the top area of the bed on your graph paper and the three sides which will hang down. My personal preference is to include the top area of the quilt which falls under the pillow area as another side. This area will most likely be hidden from view under the pillows so by treating it as the fourth side, I am able to center the design area on the bed and give the quilt better balance when it is not on the bed, but rather is hanging on a wall or for display. (Figure 4-2)

BLOCK SETTINGS USED IN QUILT DESIGNS

BLOCK TO BLOCK WITH NO SASHING: This type of quilt is fairly straightforward. You may take one block or a combination of blocks and place them in rows to fill the area you want to fill. (Figure 4-3) You have the option of filling the area that sits on the top of the bed and filling the overhang with borders (frames) or you may carry the blocks right out to the end of the quilt. In either case you would take the given area and divide it to see how many and what size blocks will fit. Example: You have an area across the top of a queen-size bed which is 60" x 80". Your quilt could consist of 10" blocks with 6 across and 8 down. You could also use 20" blocks, three across by four down. Sometimes you can figure this easily in your head but other times, it helps to mark off the graph paper in equal intervals.

The blocks used in this type of quilt can be identical patchwork blocks. You would want to see how two of the same blocks would look next to each other. It may be that a secondary design is formed by putting several blocks together, which you can enhance with different fabrics. (Figure 4-4)

Figure 4-3

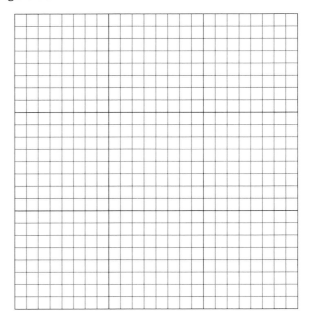

Figure 4-4

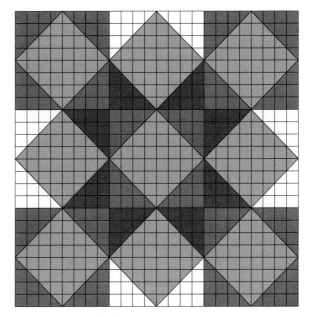

9 - 8" Four Patch

Figure 4-5

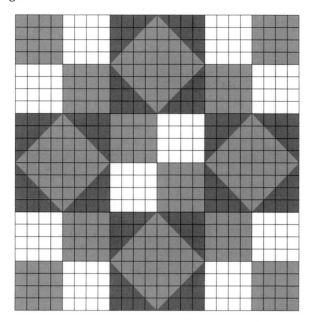

ALTERNATING BLOCKS: The blocks put together can be two different blocks which interact well together. Usually you would want to stay within the same "grid" in order to achieve secondary designs, as seen in Figure 4-5.

You can alternate a pieced block (or applique for that matter) with a solid square of fabric which can be quilted with some intricate quilting,which is shown in Figure 4-6. When working out your designs, remember to leave areas open which will allow you to show off your quilting.

Whenever alternating blocks, I always design around ODD numbers of rows across and down so that my design will have a balanced look and remain centered. (Figure 4-7)

Figure 4-6

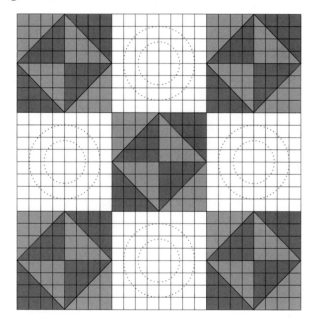

Figure 4-7

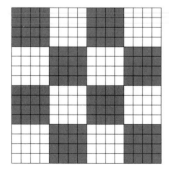 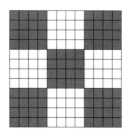

Even numbers   *Odd numbers*

DIAGONAL WITH NO SASHING: Blocks can take on entirely new looks when set on the diagonal. There are two different ways in which you can place blocks on the diagonal.

Figure 4-8: You will see that this example has one square in the corner and continues with successive odd numbered rows. Once the quilt arrives at its desired width, the rows can continue at that number of blocks until the desired length is achieved and then decreased successively.

Figure 4-9: This type of diagonal set begins with two blocks in the first row and continues adding two blocks to each row and continues with even numbered rows until you lengthen the quilt beyond a square, in which case the rows become odd numbered. The rows then return back to even numbers.

You can set identically pieced blocks together. You can set two different pieced blocks of the same grid. You can set one pieced block with a solid block.

Figure 4-8

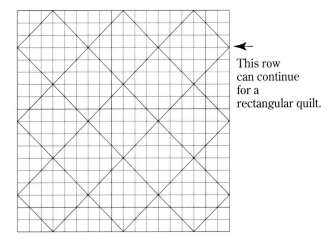

← This row can continue for a rectangular quilt.

Figure 4-9

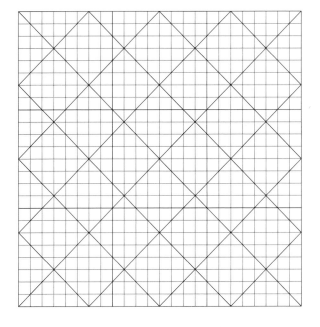

Figure 4-10

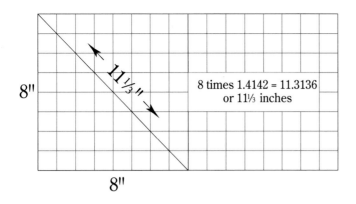

8 times 1.4142 = 11.3136
or 11⅓ inches

Figure 4-11

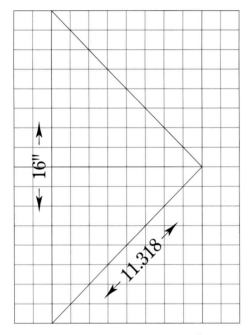

16″ ÷ 1.4142 = 11⅓″

FIGURING DIAGONAL MEASUREMENTS

The *important* number that you want to remember when dealing with the *diagonal* is 1.4142. When you are drawing on your graph paper to scale, you only need to count the number of blocks across the grid to figure out your inches. However, when the line runs diagonally across the graph paper, you *cannot* count the squares to figure out your measurement. You need to use the 1.4142 number. The formula to figure out the length of the diagonal across a right angle isosceles triangle or square is the length of the side times 1.4142. (Figure 4-10)

Conversely, if the measurement that you *do* have is the length of the diagonal line across the right angles isosceles triangle (two equal sides and one right angle), you can determine the approximate measurement of the short side by *dividing* the diagonal measurement by 1.4142. (Figure 4-11)

You can use the graph paper in two ways when drawing a diagonal set quilt.

Example 1. Drawing your lines on the diagonal to create your blocks. To determine your block size you would need to take the length diagonally across the blocks and divide by 1.4142 to determine your block size. In the following example, if each square equals 1" and there are 12 squares diagonally across the block, you would divide 12 by 1.4142 and get 8.485362749. Obviously, I used a calculator to arrive at this number. Since calculators use tenths and rulers use sixteenths, you would simply round your answer off to the nearest 16th or 8.5". Therefore, these blocks would be made 8½". (Figure 4-12)

Example 2. Drawing your lines straight along the grid for your block size. In this example I have drawn my blocks along the straight lines of the graph paper and can count the squares to determine that each block is going to be 8". The measurement that I need to determine is the length of the triangles along the outside edge. Since I know the measurement of the short side is 8", I would multiply 8 times 1.4142 to determine the length to be 11.3136 or 11⅓". If I then multiply 11.31 times two (there are two triangles on the outside edge) I would learn that the size of the piece would be 22.62 inches. It may be that when working with the graph paper that you find yourself using the 1.4142 formula in both ways to determine your measurements. (Figure 4-13)

Figure 4-12

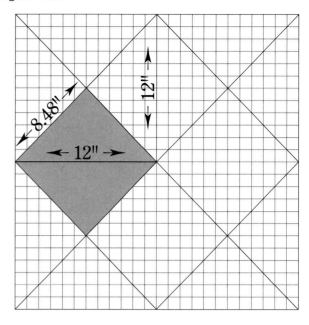

Figure 4-13

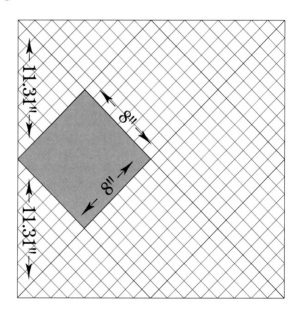

Figure 4-14

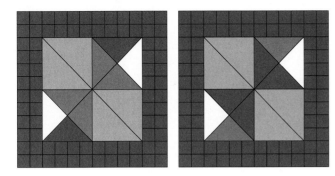

Figure 4-15

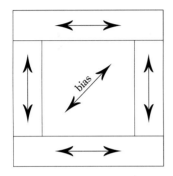

TRICK

There are books which list possible block sizes and quilt setting with or without sashings for a desired quilt size. The title of one such book is *Taking the Math Out of Patchwork* by Bonnie Leman and Judy Martin. They do the figuring for you and you can just draw the quilt to scale on graph paper.

BLOCKS SET ON THE GRID WITH SASHING

You begin in the same manner by drawing up your needs on the graph paper, with any limitations noted, and then experimenting with different size blocks and sashings to fill the area. Begin with a possible block size and number across and down the quilt to fill less than the area. Then experiment with the size sashing you can use to fill that area. Since a typical bed is longer than it is wide, you will have to either have more rows down, than across or adjust your sashing size and be creative in some other way to take up the length. One of my favorite ways to pick up extra length on a quilt is to add a row of 4" flying geese across the top and another across the bottom. This allows me to design the central area on top of the bed in a square rather than a rectangle. Other times I have added just a solid strip of solid fabric, where a nice quilting design can be highlighted.

Since each of the blocks will be "framed" by sashing they will not interact with each other. Each block will stand on its own. For this reason, quilts with a variety of blocks, such as sampler quilts, often are set apart with sashing. The sashing may be a solid piece of fabric, pieced strips of fabric or a pieced unit. Remember, though, that sashing will act as a frame around each block so you will not want it so busy that it will detract from your blocks.

Remember to take into consideration what fabric a block will be "framed" or sashed with when deciding on color. If you use a fabric along the outside edge of the block which is the same fabric that it is going to be sashed with, it will look as if one is part of the other and your design will be interrupted. You may, however, have the same fabric meet the sashing at a point and not lose the design. (Figure 4-14)

DIAGONAL WITH SASHING: If some of your blocks have been made so that some of the outside edges happen to be on the bias, you can anchor these stretchable edges down and keep them from stretching by adding a straight grain sashing. This alternative gives you another design possibility or maybe a problem solver. Of course, blocks with outside edges that are straight grains can also be sashed. (Figure 4-15)

BORDERS AND SASHINGS

Borders are generally the units, pieced or solid, which surround the entire quilt. Sashings are the units, pieced or solid, which separate block units. Because borders and sashing are such integral parts of so many quilts, this is probably a good time to discuss some possibilities. Borders and sashings act to separate, enhance or complicate. Some border possibilities are:

• Solid or mini-print fabric intricately quilted acts as a nice resting place from busy patchwork.

• Busier fabric can separate blocks and add texture or interest to the quilt.

• Striped fabrics draw your eye and complicate at the same time.

• Dark fabric can give the impression of a framing unit around a quilt or block. (Figure 4-16)

• Successively pieced blocks can create a bordering effect. (Figure 4-17)

• Alternating solid and pieced borders can act as a border. (Figure 4-18)

• Pieced borders based on a grid can be used. These are designed just as if you were designing squares on the grid, but you would draw up a border length. For example, a 3" wide border that is 60" long could accommodate design of twenty blocks that are 3" x 3".

Your borders and sashings are an important part of your quilt so you need to use your imagination when developing them.

Figure 4-16

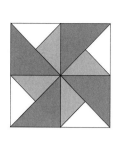
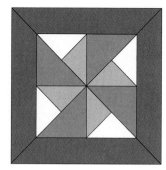

Figure 4-17

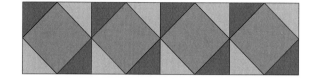

Figure 4-18

Figure 4-19

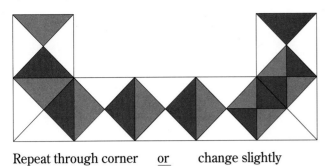

Repeat through corner   <u>or</u>   change slightly

CORNERS

Turning corners with pieced borders can be accomplished as long as units fit evenly. (Figure 4-19)

If the units do not fit evenly and you can't turn the corner with a pieced border, you can substitute something else (a solid square, a coordinated pieced block, etc.) (Figure 4-20)

You can design your pieced border so that the corners turn nicely and the pieced border meets in the middle of the sides and has an alternative element to fill in the exact space left.

The following examples show a pieced border where a substitute corner is used and another where the border meets in the middle of a side with a substitute meeting place. (Figure 4-21)

Figure 4-20

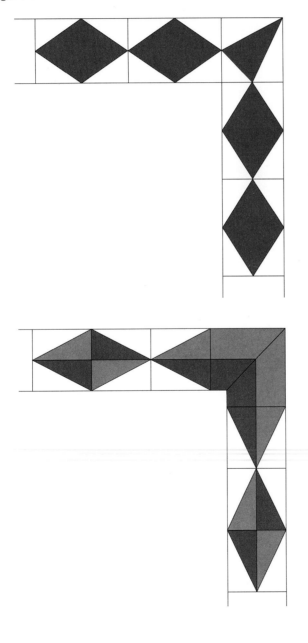

Figure 4-21

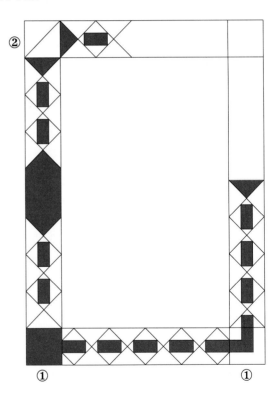

MEDALLION QUILTS

These quilts are different from the others in that they are quilts with a central focus which radiates out. You would begin in the same manner, drawing your quilt limitation out on graph paper, but instead of dividing the area into a certain number of blocks and sashings to fit, your next step would be to find the center of the top of your quilt.

Remember, by having the number of inches on the top of your bed under your pillow area the same as your side drop areas, you have decreased the size of your design area on the top of your bed.

If you use the standard Queen Size Comforter size of 84" x 92" and you subtract the area at the top of the bed, which is 60" x 80", you are left with 24" (12" drop on each side) and the 12" drop of the foot of the bed in length. If you are going to treat the pillow area the same as the sides and foot area, you need to deduct 12" from the 80" top length, which would leave you with a design area 60" wide by 68" long. (Figure 4-22)

Now you want to locate the center of this area to begin. It is helpful to just draw a light diagonal cross through this area so you are always in tune with the center. You may begin your design with a square and add extra features to the top and bottom 4" area later, or you may want to begin right away with a rectangle and work out. Once you have determined the middle of your design area, you are ready to begin filling in the area working from the middle to the outside edge. (Figure 4-23)

Figure 4-22

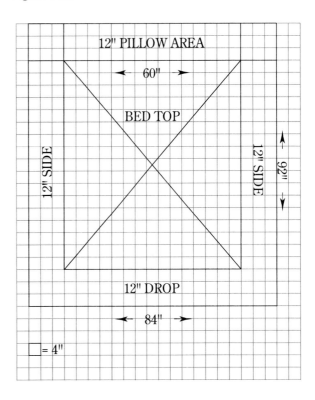

Figure 4-23

The easiest way to find the middle of any square or rectangle is to draw two diagonal lines to see where they intersect. (Figure 4-24)

Figure 4-24

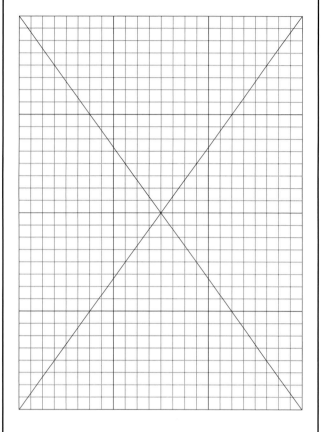

•

If you are going to do something spectacular, do it in the middle where it will get everyone's attention.

•

Use your tiny intricate piecing in the center area where you will have to do only a little bit of it. If you save it for the outside border area, you will have too much to do and it will not get the attention it deserves.

SOME MEDALLION QUILT IDEAS: An intricate block which radiates out can be your center focal point.

You can begin by placing traditional blocks which interact and add borders or areas around them to be filled in by patchwork or intricate quilting designs.

I keep writing, "You can, you can." I am throwing out just a fraction of the "you cans." It never ceases to amaze me how many wonderful ideas brand new quilters come up with when designing blocks and quilts. They are not hemmed in with the "traditional" and "what is expected." My very first quilt was a Dresden Plate quilt placed on large blocks of each of the fabrics used in the plates and contrasting borders. My quilting teacher asked, "Whatever gave you the idea to do it that way?" My answer had to be ignorance. I had never seen a traditional Dresden Plate quilt where each plate was placed on a white background, so I didn't know what was expected of me.

Not everything should be little patches; you want to leave areas open to show off the quilting and bring a soft design element into your quilt.

Again, your most valuable tool here is a blank piece of graph paper. Don't be afraid to jump right in. Initially, just shade your design in with varying degrees of pencil to get the sense of the design. When you see something you like, you can add colored pencils or fabric swatches. This is only step one of the design process. You still have color, fabric type and quilting to include in your design, all of which will add detail and interest. It is not necessary to make your design overly complicated at this stage.

Some basic design concepts you can use when making Medallion type quilts:
• Have your center area large enough to command the quilt. A tiny little 12" block in the center of a 60" area will look lost. Close to one-third of the space is a good area to consider as the center unit of the quilt.
• Have your center heavy looking or dark.
• Have your center appear to radiate out.
• Include elements of the center colors or design in areas around the center in new ways.
• Use the same design or color in the four corners, or the middle of the sides, to draw the eye out from the center.
• Create borders which use the same shapes used in the patchwork center.

ONE-TEMPLATE QUILTS

Common shapes such as squares, triangles, rectangles, hexagons and others can be repeated to make quilts. Subtle quilts are most often done in scrap fashion; and one piece is added to the other until the desired length and width is arrived at. In these cases it is not necessary to draw the quilt up on graph paper.

If, however, you would like to have a definite color or fabric interaction in this type of quilt, you would want to draw it up on graph paper so you will have a plan to follow.

SOME POSSIBLE ONE PIECE QUILT SHAPES: Your quilt does not need to be plain looking because you are only using one shape, note Figure 4-25. By changing the color placement, you can create wonderful overall designs.

Once the graph paper is used to outline the particular overall shape you are going to make, you can simply color the design in to gain the desired pattern. You would then cut your fabric pieces to correspond with your plan. (Figure 4-26)

Figure 4-25

Figure 4-26

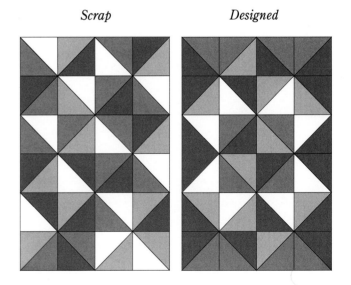

Scrap   *Designed*

Figure 4-27

WHOLE QUILT DESIGNS

There are some quilts which do not rely upon a combination of blocks in a grid or a diagonal setting. These quilts rely upon the design of the entire quilt as drawn on graph paper. Some examples of these types of quilts which come to mind are the Amish Square Within A Square (Figure 4-27) and Amish Bars (Figure 4-28).

Not all quilts need to rely on the block for their existence.

Figure 4-28

TRICK

Use a complicated traditional block and use it as the basis for the entire quilt surface.

Figure 4-29

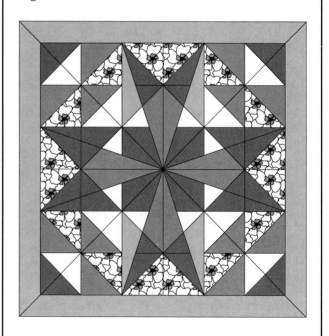

MAKING THE MOST OF
YOUR GRAPH PAPER

Before I leave this subject, I would like to encourage you to become very friendly with you graph paper, ruler, pencil and eraser. These are the beginnings of your patchwork and an open mind here and a willingness to change and play around with concepts should yield some wonderful ideas. The more you work with the graph paper the more comfortable you will become and the more innovative your patchwork. You will understand the quilt or block that you have drawn and it will actually be more comfortable for you to work with than one which is foreign to you.

Once your pattern is drawn to scale you can take each section of your quilt and draw it full-size on graph paper to make your templates (pattern pieces). Of course, large pieces like solid borders do not require templates. You can take the dimensions for these areas off your scale drawing on graph paper and mark and cut them accordingly.

Your graph paper is your game plan. It is what you intend to do. Anytime it is not necessary for me to commit myself and cut something before I am ready to use it, I don't. The reason I don't is that I want the wonderful option of changing my mind. Sometimes as a quilt develops in fabric I see a need to change something I am not happy with. If I have not already committed myself by cutting the fabric, I still have that fabric to use in a different way if I choose. Any changes I make along the way can be noted on my graph paper and the effects they might have on another area of the quilt noted. Sometimes the change happens because I placed something the wrong way and decided I liked that option better or because I see things differently on a different day. Keep the doors open for change.

You can extend the life of your graph paper and facilitate the use of grids and designs by taping a piece of tracing paper over your graph paper and shading the design in on the tracing paper with pencils.

You can get ready to go by drawing up a whole set of standard type blocks that you have divided up into all the grids. Then, by taping tracing paper over each block, you can draw many different designs. Another possibility – draw one design on tracing paper for a specific grid like a nine patch. Put that one aside and draw another nine patch up on the same size block of a different design and put one piece of tracing paper on top of the other to see if you can come up with a great design which combines the elements of both. Still another idea is to take two blocks and interlock them together into a design. The possibilities are endless. (Figure 4-30)

Figure 4-30

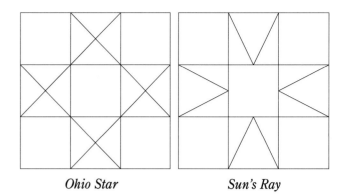

Ohio Star   *Sun's Ray*

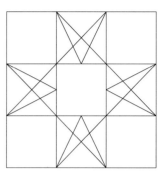

Combination of both

Graph paper is the structured form from which all your designs become a reality. It has no limitations and offers endless possibilities, but is only the beginning. The drawing that you see on the graph paper shows only the design and possibly color, if you shaded it in with colored pencils. The fabric selections you choose will add quite a bit of interest by adding texture and your quilting can serve to enhance and complicate. You don't need to make your design so complicated that the addition of interesting textures and pretty quilting will overcomplicate.

Chapter Five

Making Templates
For Hand Piecing

Figure 5-1

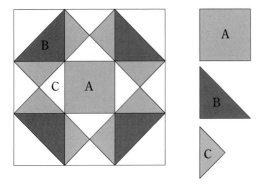

At this point, you have a design drawn either to scale or full-size and you have chosen your fabric and where you are going to use it within your patchwork. It is now time to make templates (patterns) and cut your templates out. A quick note about cutting paper and plastic. One of the surest ways to dull your good fabric scissors is to start cutting paper and plastic with them. An inexpensive pair of scissors marked "Paper" in your sewing box will be a lifesaver for your good fabric scissors.

If your design has been drawn to scale, it is now time to draw your block in full size. If you are working with a design for an entire quilt which contains several different blocks, draw full size and make templates for one block at a time so you will not be overwhelmed with pieces and confusion.

HOW MANY TEMPLATES?

Look at your block and determine how many different templates are necessary. If several pieces are the same size and shape, you need to cut only one template. One template may be used to cut different fabrics into the same shape. Give each of your pattern pieces a designated letter so you can refer to square A, triangle B, etc. and write this letter on your graph paper. (Figure 5-1)

Figure 5-2

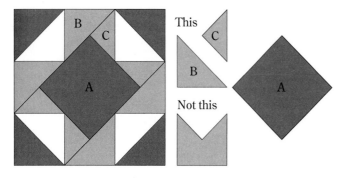

Figure 5-3

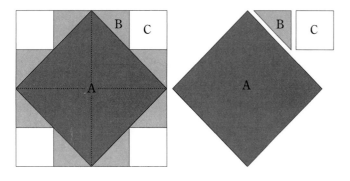

Figure 5-4

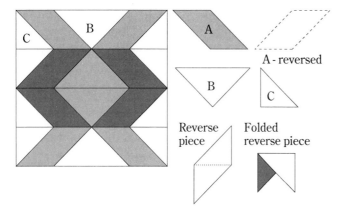

Figure 5-5

Give some thought to how the block can most simply be pieced, that is with seams that are straight lines or with the least severe angles. You will be joining pieces into units or rows and rows and units into whole blocks and then blocks into quilts.

Sometime it will be easier for you to sew together two pieces of the same fabric rather than make one template in order to make your piecing more comfortable. The C piece can be sewn at the corners and the larger B pieces can be attached to the opposite corners to eliminate any sharp angles. (Figure 5-2)

By the same token, sometimes it makes sense to make your templates larger than what the grid lines indicate when the larger piece allows you to eliminate a seam and still not have to sew any sharp angles. (Figure 5-3)

REVERSE TEMPLATES

Some pattern pieces (such as rhomboids) with angles have a right side and a reverse. It is only necessary to cut one template. To make the reverse pieces, you simply turn the template over when marking your fabric. You will known a piece is a reverse template if it cannot be folded in half and match. (Figure 5-4)

In Figure 5-5, these patterns can be folded down on themselves and match, therefore they are not reverse templates.

GRAIN LINES

All fabric has a lengthwise grain, a widthwise grain and a bias grain. There are more technical names for these grains such as warp (lengthwise) and weft (widthwise), but I'll stick to lengthwise and widthwise because then there will be no chance of confusion.

The length runs from cut end to cut end and has very little give. It will snap if you give it a tug. One hundred percent cotton fabric will tear straight down the length if a snip is made in the edge to begin the tear. The width runs from selvage to selvage (finished edge) and has a little more give than the length.

If you tug across the width, it will sound like a thud rather than a snap. Fabric will also tear across the width. You cannot assume, however, if you tear down the length of cotton and then across the width that you will end up with fabric which has been squared off. There are more threads running down the length than across the width and right angles will not always be the result. I mention this here because the assumption that a true square will result from tearing straight across and down is a false assumption. You can count on getting strips that are the same width and it will be up to you to "square them off" with a right angle at the ends.

Both of these grains are considered the "straight" or "the straight of the grain."

The other grain line is the bias which runs diagonally across the fabric and has a great degree of stretch. (Figure 5-6)

WHAT DO YOU NEED TO KNOW ABOUT GRAIN?

You want the grain of the fabric to work for you, not against you. If you completed a quilt and left bias edges on the perimeter you would have so much stretch that your quilt edge would ripple. *There is one rule with reference to grain that is hardly ever broken: never leave bias edges on the finished edge of your project.* Everything else with regard to grain is somewhat negotiable. The stretch in the bias grain will help you when you need to piece curves or applique round pieces.

When you have drawn your design up on graph paper full-size, it is a good idea to mark the grain lines of your fabric right on the graph paper before making your templates. The very general rule is that you want the block to be straight on the grain. When you are sewing your block together by hand, you may sew bias edges to bias edge pieces. You will have control of the seam by pinning each end first and then continuing to pin along the bias edge. Remember when working with any bias edge that it has the ability to stretch, and must be handled with care. (Figure 5-7)

Figure 5-6

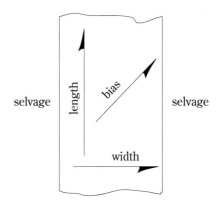

Figure 5-7

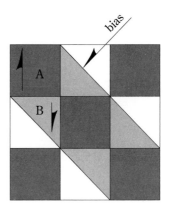

Figure 5-8

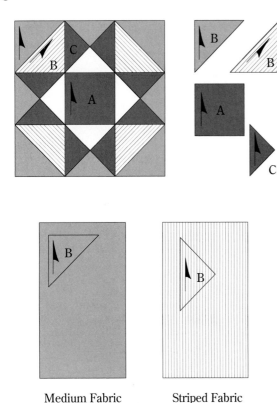

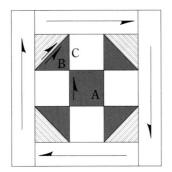

Medium Fabric   Striped Fabric

Figure 5-9

You do have creative license to change the grain lines to a degree. Consider the following block where you would like to use a stripe fabric for template B. The stripe fabric template B is set on the bias in the block. Remember that it may happen within one block that one fabric requires the straight grain of the template to go one way and in another part of the same block you will use the same template but want to make the grain go in another direction. Note this either on your key or on your template. In the following example, template B will be placed on a medium colored fabric one way and on the striped fabric another. (Figure 5-8)

If you have a design that requires that a bias edge to be on the outside, then a lattice or border on the straight grain will stabilize it. (Figure 5-9)

Decide how you are going to place your templates on the fabric from the outside of the block first and work in to the center of the block. The center of the block will be contained by the outer pieces.

WHAT ABOUT QUILTS WITH BLOCKS SET ON THE DIAGONAL? Larger areas of bias are more likely to stretch. Blocks set on the diagonal of a quilt often are done with the straight on the outside edge to avoid stretch when piecing these together. Then the entire block which has been set on the diagonal will be stabilized during the quilting process. Note that the grain on the outside triangles is on the straight with the outside edge. (Figure 5-10)

Another alternative is to piece the block so that the grain of the block sits on the straight in the quilt with the bias on the outside edge, which is then stabilized with the straight of a lattice or border. (Figure 5-11)

My personal preference is to piece the block so that the outside edge remains on the straight grain and allow the quilting to stabilize the bias.

There is more than one way to approach grain in many blocks. Choose the approach that works well for the way you plan to construct and use your block. If you have more than one block within the same quilts then be consistent in your use of grain.

Figure 5-10

Figure 5-11

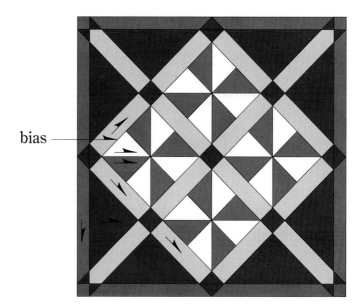

bias

Figure 5-12

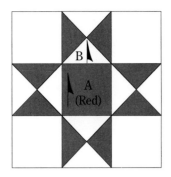

Figure 5-13

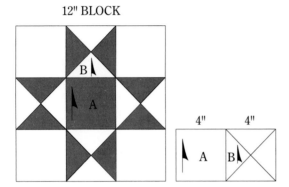

MAKING A KEY

Make a key along side your design and list each of the fabrics you have chosen to use. Under each fabric list how many of each pattern piece you need to make (Figure 5-12). This method of making the key helps to simplify the marking and cutting of fabric as you have a list to follow and fill when it is time to mark your fabric.

	Example:	White	Red
		4A	1A
		8B	8B

MAKING TEMPLATES

Your key tells you how many templates you need to make and how many of which fabric to mark. A simple way to make your templates is to place a piece of stiff see-through plastic over your graph paper and tape it down with masking tape. With a sharp pencil point, trace each pattern piece on the plastic. Resharpen your pencil when necessary to keep your markings accurate. Be sure you are marking on top of the graph paper line as you do not want your template to increase in size. It helps to trace adjoining pieces when possible as this reduces your chance of increasing the size of the template as you trace it. Once you have drawn the shapes, make your letter denotation and mark your grain lines, and cut them apart *on the line*. Remember, you are not tracing the entire block design, only one of each necessary sized shape.

You can also make templates in another way. You may cut the necessary pieces out of the graph paper with your scissors and paste them down on cardboard. Do not use water base glue as it will absorb into the paper and distort the pattern. When you have two adjoining pieces, cut them as one piece and cut them apart only after they have been pasted. The fewer times you cut around a pattern piece, the more accurate it will be. If you use this second method and your design is an involved one, it would be a good idea to draw another copy of the design so you will not become confused about how it goes back together when you are ready to sew.

If your design is a very basic one, it may not be necessary for you to draw the entire block up to full-size, but only that portion of the block that is necessary for making templates. (Figure 5-13)

REUSING TEMPLATES

Be sure to save your templates for each block in some sort of organized fashion so you may retrieve and use them again. It can be as simple as envelopes in a shoe box. You need to note the size of the block, the grid used and the pattern name or picture of the pattern.

All of my 12" blocks are stored together so when it is necessary for me to make a 12" block I only need to flip through my envelopes to retrieve a block containing the necessary templates. Several templates are interchangeable with the same grid and size block.

In the examples 5-14 and 5-15, the 12" Shoo Fly block uses some of the same template pieces as the 12" Ohio Star block.

Some templates pieces may even interchange with *different* size blocks and type of grids. For example, a 4" square for a 12" nine patch is the same as the square for a 16" four patch. (Figure 5-16)

Figure 5-14

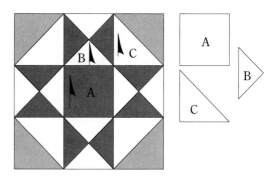

12" Ohio Star

Figure 5-15

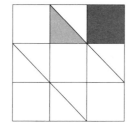

12" Shoo Fly

Figure 5-16

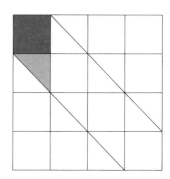

Chapter Six

Marking and Cutting Fabric

Figure 6-1

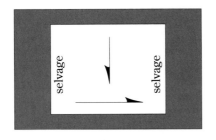

SURFACES FOR MARKING

Now that you have very carefully made templates for your patchwork, it is time to mark your fabric. Your fabric should already have been washed, dried and ironed and now should be placed on a surface which will grab the fabric as you mark. You can make a very nice marking board from wood or plywood covered with a piece of heavy, canvas-type fabric. A large piece of fine sandpaper glued to a piece of board works nicely too. It will help you a great deal to use a surface which will not allow the fabric to move as it is being marked.

STRAIGHT GRAIN AND MARKING

We need to talk about the fabric grain again. Remember, cut end to cut end is the length of the fabric (it will snap if you will tug that way), selvage to selvage is the width (it will thud and roll slightly if you tug) and diagonally is the bias, which has the greatest amount of stretch. Lay your fabric down in front of you with the wrong side up so that the selvages are running vertically. (Figure 6-1)

If you always place your fabric down this way you will instinctively know how the grain is running in your fabric and if you should want to place your templates differently in order to cut the fabric with the grain going in another direction, it will be necessary for you to move only the template and not the fabric.

TEMPLATE PLACEMENT

Each of your templates should have a straight grain line marking. This line can coincide with either the length or the width of the fabric. (Figure 6-2)

Place the template down on the wrong side of the fabric and have the wrong side of the template facing you. I know, you didn't even know your template could have a wrong side. When you made your markings on your template piece, that marked side is the right side, the other unmarked side is the wrong side.

Now it will not make any difference which side of the template you use for some pattern pieces such as squares, rectangles and isosceles triangles (two sides equal) but on some pieces (reverse pieces such as those shown below), it will make a difference. Therefore, when you are marking pieces, you always are looking at the wrong side of the template and the wrong side of the fabric unless you need to reverse a template. (Figure 6-3)

REVERSE TEMPLATES

Some patterns call for pieces which are identical; however, they are used in reverse. It is only necessary to make one template, trace the number of pieces you need to mark and then turn the template over and trace the number of pieces you need for the reverse. (Figure 6-4)

Figure 6-2

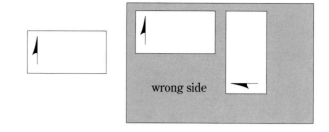

wrong side

Figure 6-3

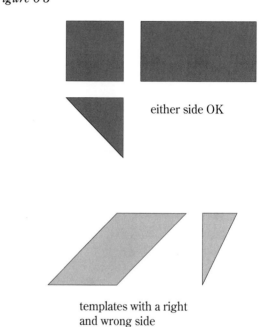

either side OK

templates with a right and wrong side

Figure 6-4

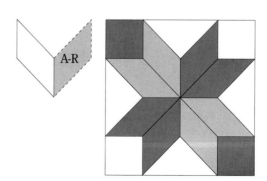

A-R

Figure 6-5

Figure 6-6

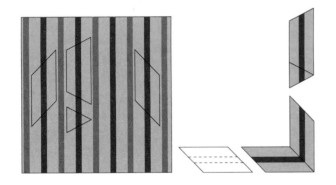

CREATIVE TEMPLATE PLACEMENT

Your placement on the fabric of the template thus far has only referenced grain or reversal; however, if you are using a stripe fabric or a fabric with a large print, such as a stylized paisley, you can place your templates very specifically to take advantage of a particular item and add interest to your patchwork. (Figure 6-5)

Stripes which meet at an angle can create an interest and draw your eye around an area. Stripes can be used to create interest in your patchwork by suggesting that your eye follow a particular direction. You can draw right on your template a particular location of where the lines begin. By making these "placement markings" on your template you will be sure that each piece of fabric is identical. (Figure 6-6, 6-7)

Figure 6-7

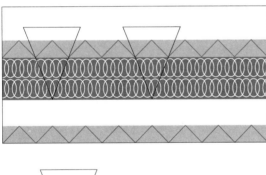

Template markings

Evening Star

A particular design can be centered in the middle of a template in order to add interest. Again, you can trace around this design right on your template so that when you move the template along your fabric to trace another it will be consistent with the previous pieces. (Figure 6-8, 6-9)

Look at stripes and large prints to see where you can add this type of customized approach to your patchwork or applique.

Figure 6-8

Template

Figure 6-9

Eight Pointed Star

Intricate paisley fabric

Template markings

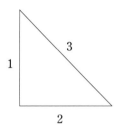
WHAT SHOULD YOU USE TO MARK YOUR FABRIC?

To answer that question fully let me tell you what the marking tool must accomplish.

• You need to be able to see your markings.

• Your line needs to be firm and not smudge, run or bleed through to the front.

• The color from the marker should not be picked up by your thread.

• Your lines should not rub off or disappear before you get to sew.

To be able to fill all of those criteria I have come to rely on the following marking tools:

• No. 4 Hard Lead Pencil – This is used on all fabrics unless the fabric is so dark I cannot see the line. I am probably using a light colored thread for piecing so the No. 4 pencil will not discolor my thread while I am piecing.

• No. 2 Pencil – If the back of the fabric has become so dark that I can no longer see the No. 4 pencil, I switch to the No. 2 pencil. My sewing thread will pick up some carbon, however I have also switched to a dark thread for piecing so the fact that the thread may be discolored is no longer a concern.

• White colored pencil – If the back of the fabric is so dark (solid black, navy, etc.) that I can't see a lead pencil at all, I switch to a regular white colored pencil. These are not chalk, but standard colored pencils.

• Yellow or silver colored pencils – If the back of the fabric is particularly busy, a yellow pencil or silver pencil is helpful.

MECHANICS OF MARKING

• Place fabric on a "grabbing" surface.

• Make certain fabric is wrong side up.

• Make certain fabric selvages are running vertically.

• Select on appropriate marking pencil.

• Place template with the wrong side facing up, except for reverse pieces where the right side is facing up.

• Make certain the grain line is going correctly as indicated on the template.

Now that you have done the above you are ready to hold your pencil at a 45° angle and mark. Do not try to go around the corners but instead mark straight across so that your lines will intersect.

• Place your piece approximately ½" away from the previous piece and mark again. Remember, you are marking the sewing lines of the finished project not the cutting lines. Patchwork seam allowance is a standard ¼", so by placing your template pieces ½" apart you have allowed for ¼" seam allowance on both pieces. Just so you won't feel silly, let me tell you that every quilter at some point had those childhood instructions, "Now cut nicely on the lines" come back and has cut on the lines instead of between them. Once you make that mistake and need to re-cut pieces you probably won't do it again.

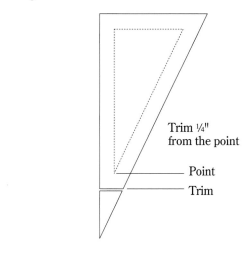

Figure 6-12

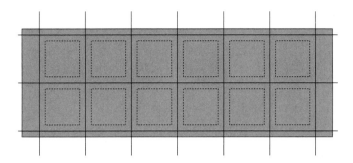

CUTTING

If you only have a few pieces to cut out, go ahead and cut them apart between the lines. Don't worry that your seam allowances might be slightly uneven. You can always trim them up as you sew each seam.

If I have a lot of pieces to cut out, I like to use a rotary cutter and a heavy plastic strip ruler.

The rotary cutter is a tool which has become a big part of quilting. It is a round razor blade which can be pushed through several layers of fabric to cut very exact straight lines. With the cutter, you will want to use a "self healing mat" on which you can place your fabric and a heavy duty plastic ruler. There are many brands out on the market for these purposes.

With one sweep, you can cut an entire row. With one sweep, you can also destroy an entire row. The rotary cutter and strip ruler probably come right after the graph paper in terms of importance to me. The rotary cutter is such a time saver that it is well worth it to learn to use it well. Go slowly at first and ask for instruction on its proper use and handling. (Figure 6-12)

SMALL PATCHWORK: When you are marking and cutting very tiny patchwork pieces, an oversized seam allowance will make handling the pieces somewhat easier and will make them less likely to be distorted during the sewing process. The extra fabric can be trimmed away after the patchwork has been sewn.

TRICK

TIPS FOR USING THE ROTARY CUTTER:

• Rotary cutters come in small and large sizes. The large size works best for cutting several layers and strips. The small cutter works best for cutting curves and smaller units and up to four layers.

• Grasp the cutter in your hand so that the end of the handle is resting in your palm. Wrap your fingers around the handle, allowing your index finger to rest on the top.

• Using a heavy plastic ruler or guide, run the blade from the bottom to the top against the edge of the ruler.

• If you find that you are not getting clean cuts, it may be that you are not putting enough downward pressure on the cutter. Dull cuts could also be caused by a nick in the blade. If that is the case, replace the cutter blade.

• If you find that your guide is moving as you cut, you may be pushing too hard against the ruler.

• This is a *very* sharp instrument. It should always be in the closed position when not in use. Store away from curious children.

LAYING YOUR BLOCK OUT

Plastic coated freezer paper has found a home with many a quilter, and not for storing hamburger. Large rolls of plastic coated freezer paper can be found in most supermarkets and quilters have found many innovative uses for this product.

As each fabric piece is cut, place it in its position right side up on the shiny side of plastic coated freezer paper. If you are making several of the same block, you only need to lay out one block at a time. Now you can see what the design is going to look like with the seam allowances. Remember that when the block is sewn together it will look much smaller. Turn your iron on cotton setting with no steam. (I like to use my old iron for this. Some of the plastic coating gets on the iron occasionally.) Place the iron on the fabric only and press, the pieces will adhere to the paper and stay in place until you are ready to sew them together. The pieces will peel off so they can be sewn together and then can be straight pinned back down on the paper. The same piece of freezer paper can be used several times before it will no longer hold. The paper can be rolled up, by itself or with several other layers of freezer paper. The advantage to this method is two fold.

• You are always ready to piece at a given moment.

• You will not have to rely on memory as to how the block goes together. If you are doing several of the same block, the extra pieces can be stored in plastic bags and taken out to correspond to those pieces which have been laid out on the freezer paper.

Many rulers designed for use with the rotary cutter have a ¼" line which runs the length of the ruler. If you place this line on the pencil marking of your fabric piece, you are cutting on the edge of your ruler which is exactly ¼" away. Therefore, you will have very consistent seam allowances. (Figure 6-13)

Figure 6-13

Figure 6-14

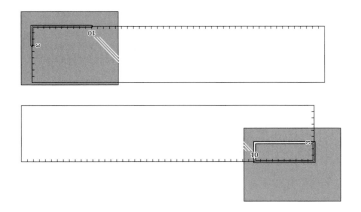

MARKING AND CUTTING BORDERS, SASHING OR LATTICE

SHORT BORDERS, SASHING OR LATTICE: Strips used in borders, sashing or lattice do not need templates; however, it is important that they are marked and cut just as carefully.

Let's say you have a short strip of fabric that is 3" x 10" to mark and cut. You can use the ruler commonly used with the rotary cutter to mark accurate pieces. (Figure 6-14)

LONG BORDERS, SASHING OR LATTICE: Long strips can be marked by two methods.

First, you can tear a length of all cotton fabric and then mark your seam lines. When tearing, I always tear the strip 1" wider than the desired width as the edges will ripple some and should later be trimmed away. (Figure 6-15)

Another method is to mark the length of the strip by moving the large ruler or a yardstick down the fabric to the desired length and cutting ¼" away from the line with scissors or a rotary cutter. (Figure 6-16)

Figure 6-15

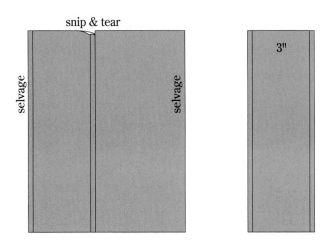

Figure 6-16

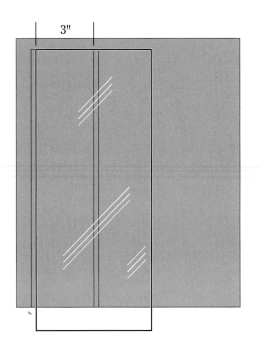
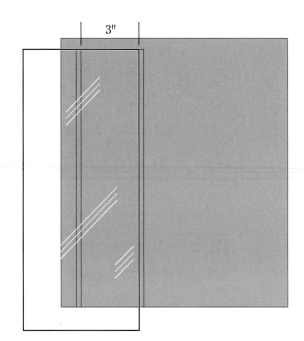

Figure 6-17

MARKING STRIPED FABRICS FOR A BORDER, SASHING OR LATTICE: When using striped fabric, I do not mark a cutting line or tear the fabric as the markings or the torn line just might not coincide with the printed stripe. What I do use is the stripes printed on the fabric as my lines to sew or cut. A deviation in size will not be nearly as noticeable in your patchwork as will be a deviation from the stripe.

MARKING LARGE SQUARES: When it is necessary for me to mark and cut large squares of fabric I don't try to rely upon my ruler to mark and cut true squares. I take the time to make a template out of graph paper and mark around it.

Recently, large plastic squares have become available on the market and have virtually eliminated my need for making larger graph paper templates. The plastic squares come in 12" and 16" sizes and allow you to cut and mark squares very easily. (Figure 6-17)

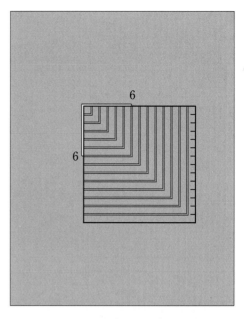

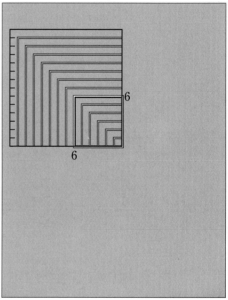

Chapter Seven

Sewing Pieces Together By Hand

NEEDLES AND THREADS

It is now time to piece (sew the patches together). You can use regular sewing thread for this – all cotton or cotton-covered polyester. The needle you use is a sharp of whatever size and type that allows you to slide the needle through the fabric easily to take nice small, even running stitches. Some quilters use quilting needles to piece and that is fine if you are comfortable using one, but that is not a rule. Some do piece with the heavier quilting thread, but again that is not the usual.

When discussing materials in this book, my goal is to give you information so that you can make your own decisions as to what to use, based on what works best for you. You may find that piecing with a sharp is just the ticket and others may find that piecing with a quilting needle works better. My aim is to give the choices and hopefully you will try alternatives and make your own decisions. If one method or tool works for you, don't fix it, but do try to keep an open mind and make your own choices.

While discussing needles it is important to tell you that both "sharps" and quilting needles (called betweens) come in sizes. You will probably want to work within the range of eights to twelves. The smaller the number the larger the needle.

THREADING NEEDLES

Did you know that large-eyed needles are available? They might be a help to anyone who has trouble with the task of threading.

Cut your thread bluntly or at an angle and do not touch the end with your fingers. Do not moisten the end. A moistened thread will stick to the needle and will actually prohibit the thread from sliding through. Resist the temptation.

Hold the needle's eye over a white surface (it makes the eye of the needle appear larger) and feed the blunt end through the eye. If it does not work after one or two tries, recut the end and try again.

If all else fails, invest in a good needle threader. This is supposed to be fun, not frustrating.

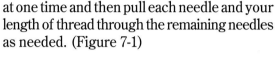

One aid that I use, especially at night when my eyes are tired, is a pair of the magnifying reading glasses you can purchase in the drugstore. These glasses make the eye of the needle much larger and easier to see and therefore easier to insert a thread through.

•

Thread a group of needles onto a spool all at one time and then pull each needle and your length of thread through the remaining needles as needed. (Figure 7-1)

Figure 7-1

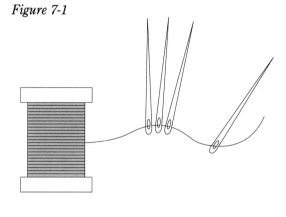

•

Right handed people should thread their needles right from the spool of thread. Left handed people should cut the thread off the spool first and then thread their needle with the end that they just cut. This practice has to do with the twist in the thread and the sewing motion which also will twist the thread. If you find that thread twists while you are sewing, dangle the needle down and let it turn to untwist itself.

Figure 7-2

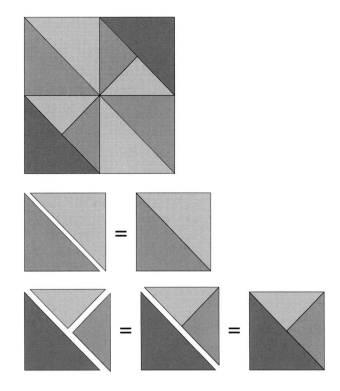

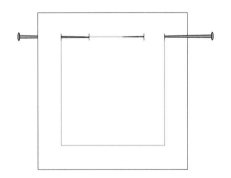

Figure 7-3

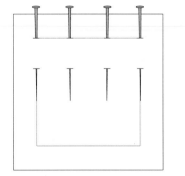

Figure 7-4

SEWING ORDER

Look at your patchwork and decide how to sew the block together in the easiest way. The easiest way is the way with the most straight seam lines and the least number of sharp angles. Sew smaller pieces together to make larger pieces. (Figure 7-2) Sew straight lines wherever possible. Sew squares into strips. Sometimes you can sew the block together in a grid, sometimes in diagonal steps and sometimes by sewing the center unit and then adding corners.

PINNING PATCHES

Did you know there are quilters' pins? Actually these are just very long straight pins with large heads. Some pins are finer than others. I like to use the longer fine pins because I can then use fewer of them; however, whatever pins you are comfortable with are fine.

In preparation for piecing, pick up the first two pieces to sew together. As a rule, I decide which seam I will begin with, flip one piece over on top of the other (right sides together) and pick the pieces up on the seam I am about to sew. If my fingers are holding the seam that I need to sew, I don't become confused as to where to pin.

• Insert straight pin in the corner of the pencil line front to back and then reinsert it along the pencil line back to front.

• Flip the fabric unit over and pin the other end in the same way. If the seam line is long, you may add more pins. (Figure 7-3)

Some quilters prefer to pin down through the pencil line. (Figure 7-4)

This is fine if you feel better about doing it this way; however, the first method will use half as many pins and therefore half as much effort to accomplish the same task.

PIECING (Sewing one piece to another)

Thread your needle with about 15" of thread (shorter if it tangles). I do not make a knot in the thread. With the fabric positioned as shown in Figure 7-5, take the pin out and insert the needle in the same place and then pull the thread through, leaving a 1" tail. Then take two to three stitches in the same place. This is called backstitching. I do not make a knot because with the backstitches in place, I could pull on the thread and it would break before it pulled out. If I make a knot, the knot would probably pull through before the thread would break. Knots are also not good because they can be hit with the needle when you are quilting and the time used to make them can be used sewing.

With the thread secured, continue sewing along the pencil line (sew on the very inside edge of the pencil line, as some marked lines can be thicker than others). Feed the fabric on the needle for several stitches before pulling the needle through. Always check the back of your work to be sure you are sewing on the pencil line and adjust the fabric with your fingers if you are not.

As you come to each pin, back out the point and hold it away from you with your hand until you reach the pin. (Figure 7-6)

After several stitches, put the needle in behind your last stitch to make a locking or backstitch. You want to do this to lock an area of stitches and to keep the line of stitching from gathering. (Figure 7-7)

As you approach the end of the piece, again back the pin point off and hold it away from you until you have actually sewn the final end. This method will hold that end point firmly together until it is sewn together. Again, take a couple of stitches in the end and cut your thread, leaving about a 1" tail. (Figure 7-8)

Figure 7-5

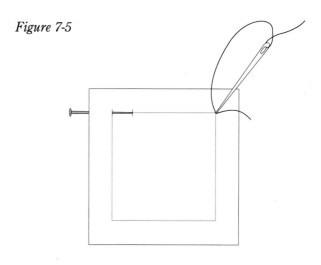

Figure 7-6

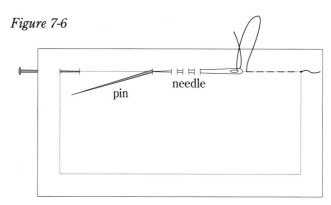

Figure 7-7

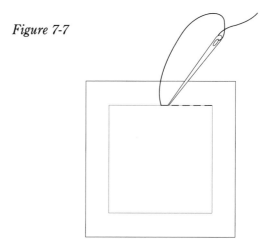

Figure 7-8

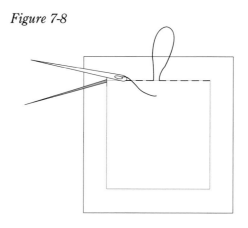

Figure 7-9

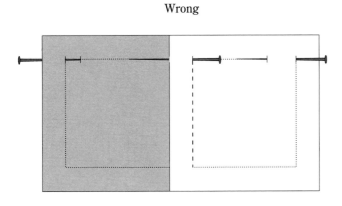

Wrong

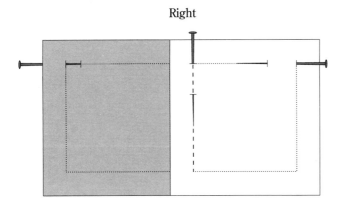

Right

Figure 7-10

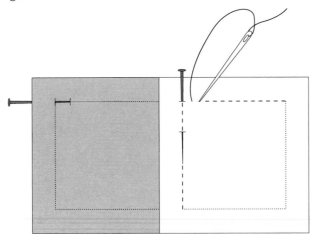

TRIMMING SEAM ALLOWANCES

If we eyeballed our seam allowances, when we cut our patches out, it may be necessary at this point to neaten up those seam allowances and trim them together. This would be the time to do that. Don't wait until the entire block has been pieced. It will be harder to hold the rest of the block away to trim and the task will be tiring. Sew and then trim, if necessary.

FINGER PRESSING

This task is a simple one and such a good habit to get into. Once your seam is sewn, fold the fabric over to expose the seam you have just sewn and fold both of the seam allowances toward the darker piece of fabric. Work your fingers along the seam to press it. This task makes that seam line nice and crisp and will aid you when joining pieces together with seams. Cotton fabrics will hold the crease much better than blends. This is one of the advantages of using 100% cotton fabric.

Place your sewn piece back down on the laid out design and pick up the next unit to be pieced.

MATCHING SEAMS

Many times it is necessary to sew two pieced pieces together and make the intersecting seams match. This takes practice. The method I use to accomplish this is as follows: the two ends of the pieces are pinned as usual; however, the place where the seams need to match is pinned vertically. If I pinned this in the regular fashion, even if the pin went in straight, the practice of pulling the pin over to pin horizontally would move the seam. (Figure 7-9)

Sew as you normally would and leave the pin at the matching place until it has been sewn. Take one backstitch going through to the other side of the seam allowance. *(Always sew through the base of the seam allowance, to allow it to move freely. Never sew seam allowance down when you are hand piecing)*. Once past the seam allowance, go straight through to the back, then straight through to the front where you can backstitch. Pull the thread tightly here and continue on down the seam. (Figure 7-10)

SEWING A SET-IN PIECE

A set-in piece may be a necessity when sewing your patchwork together and should not be feared. The angle can be slight or severe. A set-in piece can be from one template or two pieces of sewn together fabric that require you to set a piece in place. Let's deal with a one template piece first. (Figure 7-11)

At the point where you need to pivot, make a small slit in the seam allowance not quite to the pencil line. Place the right sides of the two pieces together along the first seam and pin just as if you were sewing a straight seam. Only pin one side. (Figure 7-12)

Sew as you would normally set a straight seam and end with a backstitch at the end point. Take the pin out and pivot the other end up and pin along the final line. Do not take another backstitch, but continue to sew up the final line, taking care that your very first stitch up that final line does not pinch the back piece. Once you started up the line, you have it made.

Now let's deal with two pieces which have been sewn together and now require that you add a set-in piece. It is done exactly the same way, except for the fact that it is not necessary for you to slit the fabric at the center point as your seam allowances are not sewn together and are already free. (Figure 7-13)

Figure 7-11

Figure 7-12

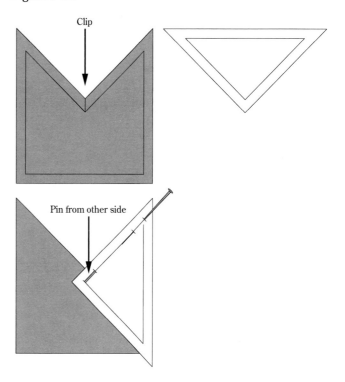

Figure 7-13

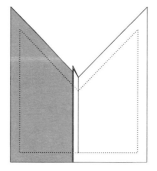

Figure 7-14

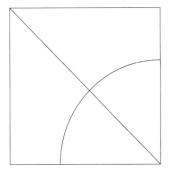

Figure 7-15

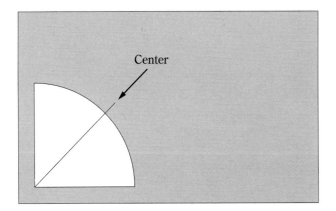

Center

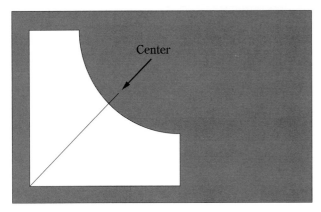

Center

SEWING CURVED SEAMS

Some patchwork has curved seams so you will need to know how to deal with them.

• Mark the center of your curved seam on both template pieces. Do this by drawing a diagonal line through the square unit. (Figure 7-14)

• Mark the center of your curved seam on both fabric pieces in the seam allowance. If you place straight sides on the straight of the grain, the curves will fall on the bias, where the stretch will help in your piecing. (Figure 7-15)

• Clip the concave fabric piece. (Figure 7-16)

• Make V-notches in the convex piece. (Figure 7-17)

• Pin the end by inserting the pin through the pencil line and perpendicular to it. (You cannot pin horizontally along a curved seam.) Next, pin the center in the same manner and add as many pins as necessary to keep that portion of those two curved lines together. (Figure 7-18)

• Sew from the end to the middle. Making sure you are sewing through both the front and back lines simultaneously, stretch and manipulate the fabric as you sew to the midpoint.

• Once you have reached the midpoint, pin the other end in the same manner as the first part and continue sewing to the end.

• Press the seam allowance against the larger piece whenever possible. This will not be possible if the color of the smaller piece's seam allowance might show through into the larger piece, in which case you would press both seam allowances to the smaller piece.

Figure 7-16

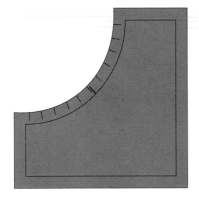

Figure 7-17

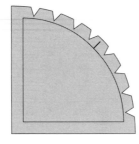

Figure 7-18

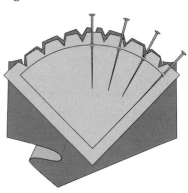

Traditional Curved Piecing Blocks

Drunkard's Path 1

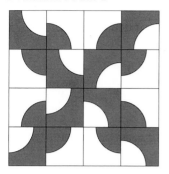

Drunkard's Path 2

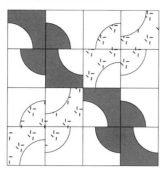

Wonder of the World

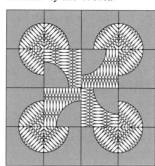

Drunkard's Path Variation

The Dove

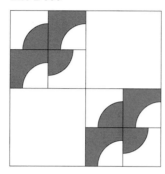

Orange Peel

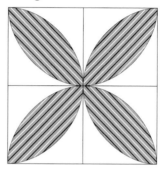

Love Ring

3-inch Template (Can be used to make 12″ 4 patch blocks.)

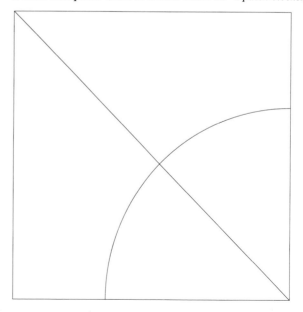

PRESSING YOUR PATCHWORK

When your block is all pieced, it is time to press it. Pressing the patchwork block correctly is very important. A steam iron and heavy pressure can really distort your block. I prefer to use a dry iron and only enough pressure to accomplish the task of making the seam allowance lie flat. Rather than dragging the iron over the patchwork, use an up-and-down motion. Looking at the wrong side, begin pressing with your seam allowances pressed to the darker side. This is a very general rule. If you feel that you need to press an allowance to another side because of too much bulk and you cannot see the allowance on the front, then by all means do! You want your block to look crisp but not shiny and flat, so press carefully. If you have several points all coming together at one place, you may trim the points in order to reduce the bulk in that one area. Consistency is the rule. Once you make the decision to press seam allowances in a certain direction, press all allowances for that block in the same manner.

TRICK

When I am pressing a group of specific size blocks at one time, I draw the finished size square right on my ironing board cover with a pencil. I place a straight pin in the four corners of the patchwork block and tack at the corner points on the ironing board. In effect, I am blocking these blocks as I am pressing them.

Chapter Eight

Other Drafting Techniques

Once you have gotten past the grid, you might want to try some other patchwork drafting techniques which will expand your creative process.

COMPASS

In this chapter, we will be using a compass along with a ruler to make some new designs. Compasses you buy at a five-and-dime store will work well for awhile, some better than others. As soon as your compass doesn't hold its place well, look for a replacement. This type of compass, even when it is working well, has a pretty short distance range.

You can also use a drafting compass with an extension arm. It works well as long as you are familiar with its capabilities, but it, too, has a fairly short range.

You can use a yardstick compass. A yardstick compass consists of two units which slide on a yardstick or ruler, one with a point and the other with pencil lead. It works well, will not loosen up and has a large range. My only suggestion would be to cut your yardstick down to about 18" and use this apparatus for most of your blocks. Using all 36" of the yardstick will sweep everything in sight off your working surface, including your cup of tea.

There is another type of compass which I have stumbled across at the local flea markets. That is the carpenter's compass. It's usually made of steel and has a solid point with a place for a stylus to fit in the other side which you can easily use for a pencil. It is heavy, comes in large and small sizes and is very sturdy. Keep your eyes open; you may just stumble across one too.

Figure 8-1

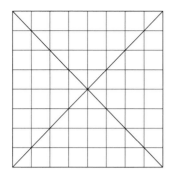

Figure 8-2

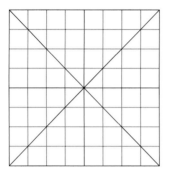

Figure 8-3

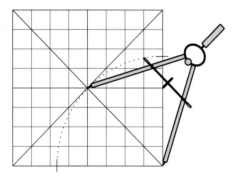

Figure 8-4

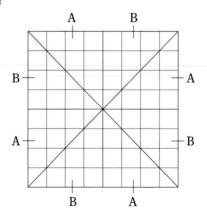

THE EIGHT-POINTED STAR DESIGN

This is another design type which can be drawn up and used to make designs and copy designs. Yes, you can make eight-pointed stars with this drafting technique, but you can also make many other designs.

To make the eight-pointed star basic outline:

• Draw up the desired size square on graph paper.

• Make two diagonal lines corner to corner to find the center. (Whenever looking for the center of a block, two diagonal lines will find it much faster than counting or measuring across and down.) (Figure 8-1)

• Make a vertical and horizontal line through the center. (Figure 8-2)

• Using a good compass, place the point of the compass on any corner and open it until the pencil just touches the center of the block. When it is set to reach the center, swing the compass to the sides of the block where it can intersect and make a slash on each side. You do not need to draw the entire arc, only indicate the measurement by a slash on the side. (Figure 8-3)

• Repeat this process on the other three corners of the block. Each side should now have two slash marks on it. Go around and mark the slashes A and B continually around the block from right to left. You are doing this so you will have a point of reference. (Figure 8-4)

- Join the A marks to B marks vertically. (Figure 8-5)
- Join the A marks to the B marks horizontally. (Figure 8-6)
- Join A marks to the B marks diagonally in each direction. (Figure 8-7)

You now have drawn the basic eight-pointed star design. If you begin in the center and follow the lines out you should be able to see eight 45° diamonds radiating out from the center. (Figure 8-8)

Figure 8-5

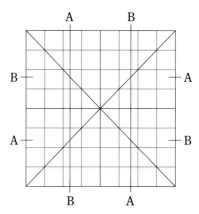

Figure 8-6

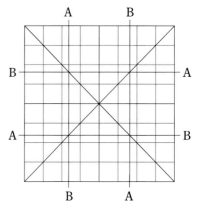

Figure 8-7

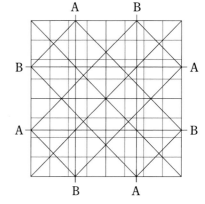

Figure 8-8

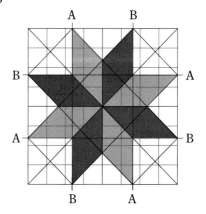

TRICK

To locate the A/B marks mathematically:

- Divide the square size by 1.4142.
- Subtract the answer from the square size.
- Measure this distance from each corner in both directions.
- Example:
  12" square divided by 1.4142 = 8.49 or 8½.
  12 minus 8½ = 3½.
  The A/B marks are 3½" from each corner.

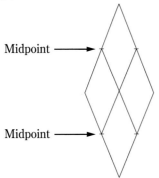

Figure 8-9

Midpoint ⟶

Midpoint ⟶

Figure 8-10

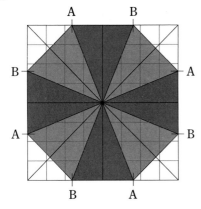

Figure 8-11

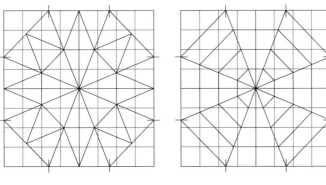

Evening Star   *Spider Web*

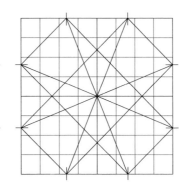

WHAT IF YOU WANTED TO MAKE EACH DIAMOND CONSIST OF MORE THAN ONE PIECE? You may take the length of each side of the diamond and divide it equally and join those points to make each diamond consist of four diamonds. (Figure 8-9)

Do you want each diamond to consist of nine diamonds? Divide each side into thirds.

WHAT ELSE CAN YOU DO WITH THE EIGHT-POINTED STAR DESIGN? If you only go as far as to find the A and B slash marks and draw diagonal lines joining the A's to A's and the B's to B's, you have drawn an octagon. You have drawn a block divided into eight sections. To complete the octagon, you would join the A marks to the B marks across the corners. The perfect octagon in a block you would like to copy is a dead giveaway that the block is an Eight-Pointed Star design. (Figure 8-10)

There are all kinds of design possibilities when dividing up each equal wedge. This type of block is also called a kaleidoscope. (Figure 8-11)

The Eight-Pointed Star design affords you the ability to work with eight equal pieces which radiate out. The rest is up to you. The same ability to copy and create designs that you found with grids is available in the Eight-Pointed Star design.

PIECING TIP

Figure 8-12

Whenever piecing a unit which goes around the center rather than up and down in a grid, always piece one half and then the other half and join the two halves. The center area where you have possibly eight seams coming together does take some skill and precision. (Figure 8-12)

When you are just beginning, try to use the same fabric for the pieces in the center rather than different fabrics so your seam lines will not be quite so obvious. As your skill improves your choices can be more varied.

Often new quilters will experience a fullness in the center of an eight-pointed star design. The cause for this is usually center templates that are slightly over-sized. If you experience this, take the seams in slightly in the center until your piece lies flat. Before making additional blocks using these templates, check their accuracy.

Figure 8-13

Dresden Plate

DIVIDING A CIRCLE

Some patchwork patterns such as the Dresden Plate, Mariner's Compass and Grandmother's Fan rely on your ability to divide a circle evenly. (Figures 8-13, 8-14, 8-15)

Figure 8-14

Mariner's Compass

Figure 8-15

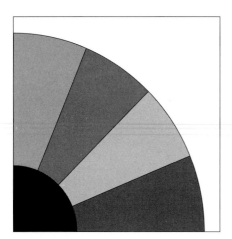

Grandmother's Fan

DRESDEN PLATE

A Dresden Plate block usually consists of sixteen wedge pieces with a curved top edge, or pointed wedges for a Fancy Dresden Plate. These wedged sections are pieced together and then appliqued down on a background square.

To draft your wedge shape:
- Draw a square.
- Make your diagonal lines to find the center.
- Place your compass point in the center and draw a circle which fills the square but leaves you room to make scallops for the traditional block or points for a Fancy Dresden Plate. (Figure 8-16)
- Divide the square vertically and horizontally. Right now, without going any further, you have divided the circle into eight pieces. (Figure 8-17)

Figure 8-16

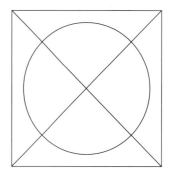

Figure 8-17

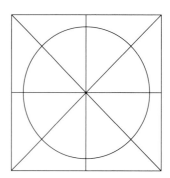

┬TRICK┬

It is not necessary for you to draw the entire square in order to accomplish this dividing technique. You can draw up a square with sides one half the measurement to develop only one quarter of the entire square. (Figure 8-18)

Figure 8-18

This is the same way you would draw the entire Grandmother's Fan block.

Figure 8-19

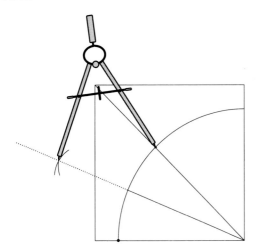

• To divide each wedge further, place the compass on the arc of the circle and make a slash beyond the circle's edge. (If you don't have room on your paper you can draw a smaller guide arc inside the circle and place the compass on it to make your slash mark.) Move the compass without changing its setting to the other side of the wedge along the same arc and make a slash long enough to intersect with the first one that you just made. Place your ruler at the point of intersection and the center point of the circle (or corner if you are working from one quarter of the block.) Draw a line to divide the wedge. (Figure 8-19)

In Figure 8-20, the example shows dividing the same wedge using the guide arc.

Figure 8-20

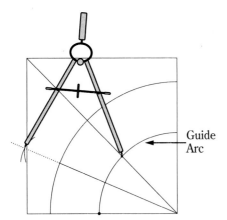

Guide Arc

SCALLOPED WEDGES: You have now divided the circle into sixteen pieces, your traditional Dresden Plate. To make the scallop on the end of the wedge, just slide a small circular item which you can trace onto the end of the wedge. Or you can reduce the size of your compass to a small circle, which will intersect with the sides of the wedge. (Figure 8-21)

POINTED WEDGES: To make a pointed wedge, divide the wedge one more time and draw one more arc and connect the lines. (Figure 8-22)

THE HOLE IN THE MIDDLE OF
THE DRESDEN PLATE: The only other thing you need to make is the small circle in the center of the Dresden Plate. This can be accomplished by placing your compass point in the center and drawing your desired size circle. If I am only drawing up one quarter of the Dresden Plate in order to make my wedge, I still draw the entire circle for the center in order to better see its actual size. Seeing only one quarter of this center circle can be misleading. (Figure 8-23)

Figure 8-21

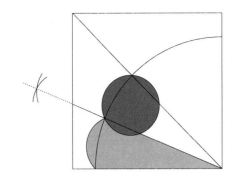

Figure 8-22

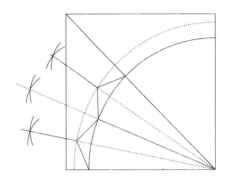

Figure 8-23

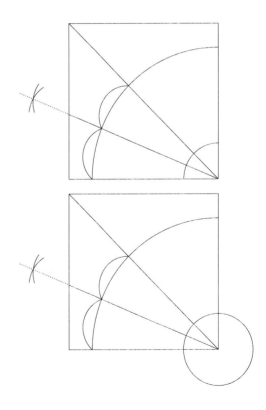

Figure 8-24

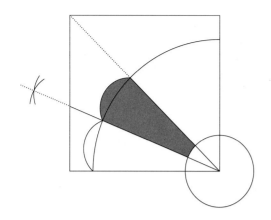

MAKING YOUR TEMPLATE FOR
THE DRESDEN PLATE: You now have the wedge shape which you need to trace in order to make your template for the Dresden Plate. The wedges are pieced together and the entire donut shape created is appliqued down on a solid square of background fabric. The seam allowance of the curved (or pointed) outside edges and the center are turned under and sewn with the applique stitch. (Figure 8-24)

OTHER USES
FOR A DIVIDED CIRCLE

You can continue to divide each wedge further by placing the compass between those points on the same arc that you want divided. (Figure 8-25)

Figure 8-25

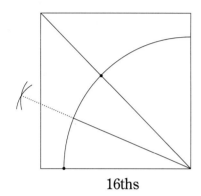

16ths

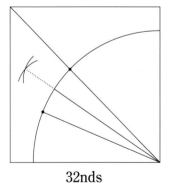

32nds

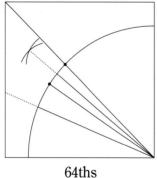

64ths

MARINER'S COMPASS: This block is created by dividing your circle many times and using your ruler to join the same points together along several arcs. This is not a beginner block but a commanding piece of patchwork and well worth the effort it involves. (Figure 8-26)

A suggestion to remember when drafting this block is to have the pieces coming into the center come back into four or eight pieces so you do not have a multitude of pieces all coming together in the middle. (Figure 8-27)

If your design does have many pieces coming together in the middle, plan to applique a circle unit on top of those pieces. (Figure 8-28)

Figure 8-26

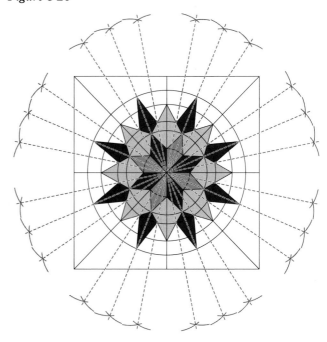

Figure 8-27

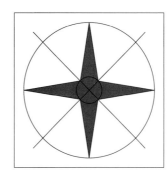

Figure 8-28

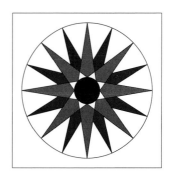

Figure 8-29

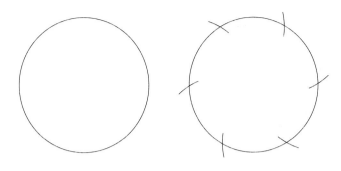

MAKING HEXAGONS: Hexagons are six equal sided units. To make a hexagon:

- Draw a circle.
- Do not change the compass setting. Place the compass point on any point of the circle and make a slash into the circle arc.
- Place the point on that slash and continue to slash the circle until you come back to the beginning. (Figure 8-29)
- Join the slash marks with your ruler, as shown in Figure 8-30.

You have just drawn a hexagon.

Figure 8-30

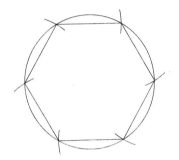

Possibilities:

• Intersect the hexagon at the slash marks to come up with some new designs such as 60° diamonds and triangles which look like three-dimensional boxes. (Figure 8-31)

• How about six-pointed stars inside a hexagon? (Figure 8-32)

Another idea:

• Draw three hexagons next to each other so they they interlock to give you some more design possibilities. The idea is to find common points to connect in order to create new patterns. (Figure 8-33)

These drafting techniques are just some more patchwork possibilities. They hold many wonderful ideas for you to experiment with. Just as you connect lines in blocks which originate from a grid, there are many designs to be made when you use an evenly divided circle or hexagon. Try them; you'll like them.

Figure 8-31

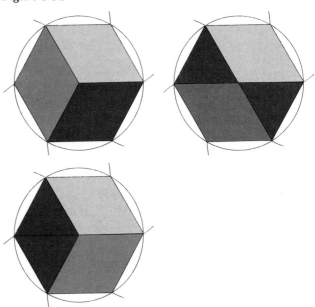

Figure 8-32

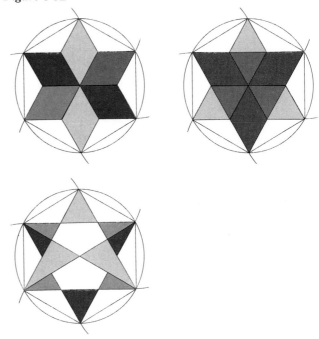

Figure 8-33

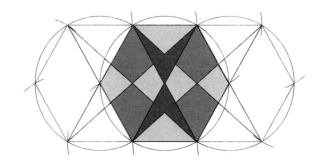

Figure 8-34

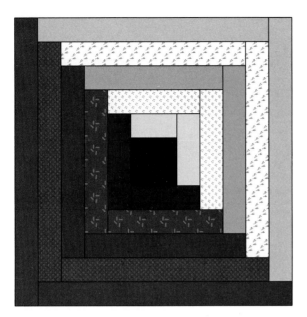

Log Cabin

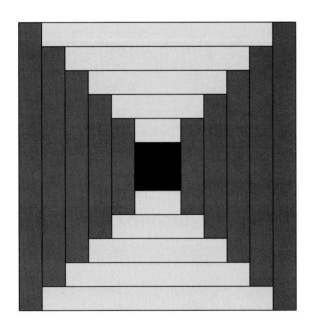

Courthouse Steps

STRIP PATCHWORK

There are some patchwork blocks which do not rely upon making templates for each piece, but rather use strips of fabrics in order to create their designs. Two traditional blocks that fall in this category are the Log Cabin and the Courthouse Steps. (Figure 8-34)

DETERMINING HOW MANY STRIPS AND WHAT SIZE: Both the Log Cabin block and the Courthouse Steps block have a central square and an equal number of strips around it. The size of the center square and the number and width of the strips will vary depending upon the finished square desired. To determine the size of the center block and the strips, begin with your desired finished block size. For the sake of our example, I will use a 12" block. If I want my center block to be 2", that means I have 5" left to divide on each side of the center square into strips. Therefore, five 1" strips would fill the area. Four 1¼" strips would fill the area as well. (Figure 8-35)

CONTRASTS IN A LOG CABIN: The Log Cabin block is traditionally done with a red fabric center to symbolize the warmth in the home or a yellow fabric center to symbolize a light in the window or hospitality. You can make your center any color you like and come up with your own special symbolism. Whatever color you choose, you will want your center to contrast with the first set of strips which will surround it.

The strips or "logs" as they are often called, are traditionally done with one side being light, to symbolize the good in life and one side being dark, to symbolize the "darker" side of life. Again, you may create your own contrasts and symbolism. Sometimes, only one fabric is used on each side, and other times this is done with several light and dark fabrics on each side. Log Cabin quilts were often done as scrap quilts, using light and dark scraps on each side.

Figure 8-35

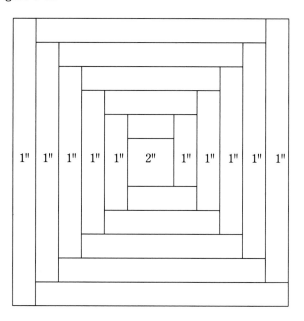

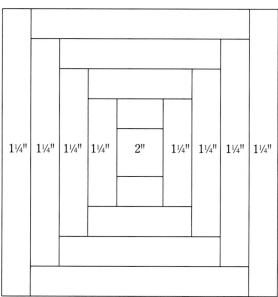

Figure 8-36

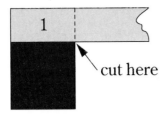

Figure 8-37

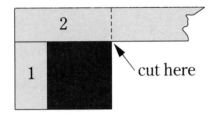

Figure 8-38

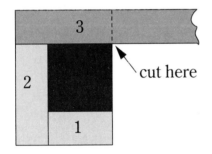

Figure 8-39

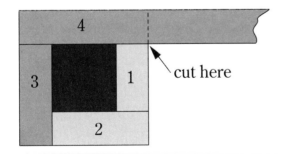

BUILDING A LOG CABIN: Once you have determined your center square size and the strip size, you will want to cut your center square, adding the ¼" seam allowance on all sides or ½" to the finished size square. Your strips are then cut ½" wider than the desired finished width and long enough to accommodate the lengths plus seam allowance. Most quilters estimate the length. If they need two strips that total about 5", they might cut a 7" strip and just trim away the excess.

Starting with your first strip on the light side, place your strip across the side of the square and sew across. The reason for starting with the light side is that the lighter fabrics appear larger than the darker fabrics and the block will end up with the longer pieces being on the dark side. This will give your block a more balanced look. Once the seam is sewn, cut off the excess portion of the strip. (Figure 8-36)

Now, working clockwise, add your next light strip across the end of the first strip and your square. Sew and trim. (Figure 8-37)

Continuing clockwise, add your first dark strip in the same manner. (Figure 8-38)

Finally, sew your next dark strip up the last side. (Figure 8-39)

You have just completed your first row around your log cabin. Continue in this manner until all your strips have been added.

A few words of caution here are warranted. The mechanics of making a Log Cabin block are simple; however, because they appear to be so simple, many quilters do not take seriously the amount of fluctuation that can be created by having seam allowances which are too big or too small. In our example, a 12" Log Cabin with five strips on each side, has TEN seams across the block. If you are sewing the strips on and you are consistently only ¹⁄₁₀" too big with your seam allowances, then you will have made an 11" block instead of a 12" block. Because this is a simple block, it is easily completed by cutting the strips using the rotary cutter and sewing them on using the sewing machine. The watchword here is to measure and cut carefully and to "pretest" your seam allowance on your sewing machine to make sure you are sewing with a ¼" seam allowance.

THE COURTHOUSE STEPS: This block is very similar to the Log Cabin and only differs in the sequence of construction. Instead of sewing the strips around the center in a clockwise motion, the strips are added to opposite sides at the same time. (Figure 8-40)

Once your blocks are completed, they can be placed in a variety of settings to achieve wonderful quilt designs using the half dark/half light contrasts.

Figure 8-40

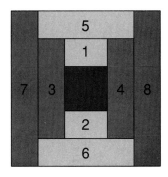

Chapter Nine

Applique

Figure 9-1

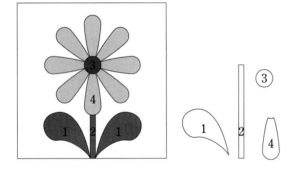

Applique is different from pieced patchwork in that the fabric unit(s) are sewn on top of one or more pieces of background fabric. This technique allows much more flexibility of design since you don't have to have individual pieces fit together like a puzzle to create a solid unit. You also don't need to be an artist. If you can find a design to trace, you can turn it into an applique.

APPLIQUE TEMPLATES

Templates for applique work are made like pieced patchwork templates. Place the plastic template material on top of the applique pattern and trace the pattern pieces. Cut the templates out on the line. Like pieced patchwork, you only need to make one template for each shape. (Figure 9-1)

MACHINE APPLIQUE

A sewing machine which can produce a close and even zigzag stitch can be used to applique pieces to a background fabric.

- Make templates for each different pattern piece.
- Trace them on the wrong side of the fabric with the wrong side of the template facing you.
- Cut out on the line (you have no seam allowance to turn under).
- Position all your pieces on the background and proceed to cover all the raw edges with a long running stitch to hold the pieces in place. You may also use a fabric glue stick or hand baste the pieces in place.
- Now, continue back over the exposed edges with a smooth zigzag stitch. It is often helpful to place a piece of tracing paper underneath the background fabric between it and the feed dogs of the sewing machine so the fabric will not bunch. The paper can easily be torn away after the sewing has been completed.

HAND APPLIQUE

Fabric – Here again let me mention that 100% cotton fabric is the preferred fabric for hand applique. The fabric will fold easily and take the crease better than a blend, allowing you to turn the raw edges under.

Grain – Use the grain of your fabric to your advantage in applique. Put the straight lines of angles along the straight grain and the curves along the bias line. (Figure 9-2)

Patterns – If you are artistic, you can draw your own patterns and then make templates of each piece.

If you are not artistic, you can trace patterns on tracing paper and then make templates of each piece. Some sources for good applique patterns are children's coloring books, greeting cards, wrapping papers, wall papers, fabrics, advertising items, etc. Start to notice the shapes around you in your everyday life as possibilities of applique patterns. I once asked my husband to stay right behind a Mayflower moving truck on an interstate highway just so I could sketch their ship logo for an applique pattern. The possibilities are endless.

Figure 9-2

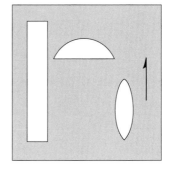

Figure 9-3

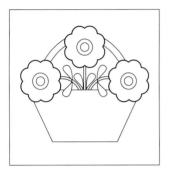

Figure 9-4

NEEDLES FOR APPLIQUE

Sharps are usually used in applique work. A nice thin needle which will slide through the edge of the fold is your goal. If you are looking for a size, I would recommend a size 10 to begin with and 11's and 12's as you gain expertise.

THREADS FOR APPLIQUE

You want to use a good cotton or cotton-covered polyester thread which matches the top fabric that you are applying. You can also use one strand of embroidery floss to better approximate color if you would like.

CENTERING ON BACKGROUND FABRIC

If your design needs to be placed on your background fabric and centered, you can press your background fabric across and then in quarters and then diagonally. The crease marks that you have made reveal the center and points of reference to center your applique work. (Figure 9-3)

FLEXIBILITY OF PLACEMENT IN APPLIQUE

There is flexibility in the placement of many applique patterns. This can be both good and bad. If you are making a one-of-a-kind, you can change the placement to fit your creativity. (Figure 9-4)

However, if you are making several units of the same applique, all the units need to be consistent and the placement uniform.

USE OF A LIGHT BOX

Some applique designs need to have the pattern pieces placed exactly in a certain place on the block so that it will go together neatly or so that several of the same blocks will be consistent with each other.

A light box can be used to transfer the lines for placement to fabric. This can be accomplished by using a see-through surface and placing a light under it so that you can trace them or actually place your pieces. This method will work with even the darkest background color. Do not use pencil for your marking on the paper plan, as pencil will not show through as well as a marker.

Using your light source, position your pattern pieces in their appropriate places (one on top of the other if needed) and baste them into place. I don't like to use pins because they will fall out, stick you at the least expected times and create just the perfect place for your thread to become tangled. This method works fine with all the methods and is the one I use when it is necessary for each piece to be positioned in an exact place. (Figure 9-5)

Figure 9-5

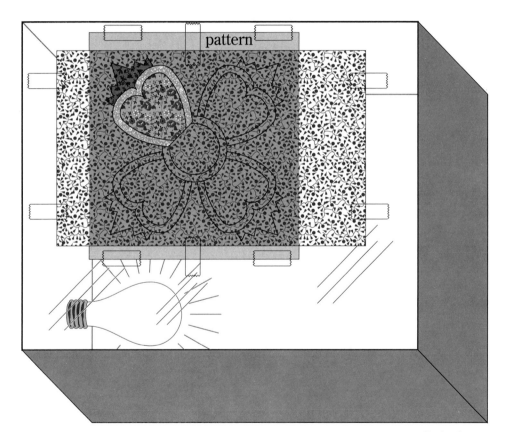

light box

METHODS OF HAND APPLIQUE

There are several methods of turning the edge under in applique and I will explain some of the more common methods, giving you each with my assessment of their pluses and minuses.

METHOD ONE – Marking On The Right Side and Basting The Edge Down

- Make a finished size template of each of your different applique pieces.
- Trace the piece on the right side of your fabric with the right side of the template facing up.
- Cut out with a scant ¼" seam allowance.
- Turn under the edge along the pencil line and baste.
- Position the piece on the background fabric; baste and applique down.

This method had only minuses for me when I was introduced to applique. The marking on the right side of the fabric meant that I not only had to turn the fabric under well, which my fingers had no experience doing, but I also had to make sure none of the lines would show.

METHOD TWO – Marking On The Wrong Side Of The Fabric And Basting

- Make a finished template of each of your different applique pieces.
- Place the template, WRONG SIDE up on the wrong side of the fabric and trace.
- Cut out with a scant ¼" seam allowance.
- Baste along marking line.
- Turn fabric edge under along basting line and baste seam allowance under.
- Position fabric to the background fabric; baste and applique down.

This method eliminates the marking on the top of the fabric, but substitutes it with another line of basting. It still requires more expertise to fold the edges under well in order to baste.

METHOD THREE – Freezer Paper Applique

- Make templates of each of your different applique pieces.
- Place your template right side up on the dull side of plastic coated freezer paper.
- Trace the template for each applique piece on freezer paper and cut out on the lines.
- Trace the template for each applique piece on the wrong side of the fabric with the wrong side of the template facing you.
- Cut the fabric piece out with a ¼" seam allowance.
- At the ironing board, lay your fabric piece down with wrong side facing up and position the corresponding freezer paper with its shiny side up within the marking lines.
- Using a cotton setting on your iron and NO steam, use the edge of your iron to fold the seam allowance over the freezer paper and press. The heat of the iron melts the plastic coating and causes the fabric in the seam allowance to adhere. Concave curves should be clipped not quite into the marking line and corners should be pressed on one side and then the other side over it. Do not clip off points as you will tuck them under when you press. (Figure 9-6)
- Position the applique pieces with the paper still inside them and the right side of the applique up on your background fabric and press the entire applique design down. The exposed freezer paper will cause the pieces to stick to each other and the background fabric. You will want to add a little basting to assure that they will hold in place until you are ready to applique.
- Once ALL the pieces are positioned, you may applique. While sewing your edges down with the applique stitch your needle will tend to bounce off the paper and sew only the fabric. If, however, you find that you have sewn through the paper, it is not a problem, as the paper will just tear through when it is removed and leave your stitch intact.
- When one piece adjoins another and goes UNDER it, you don't need to press the seam allowance on the portion that goes underneath.
- When sewing one piece which is on top of another piece (called layered applique), again, only sew through to the layer which is immediately beneath. The needle will stop at the paper unless you really force it through.
- When you are ready to trim away excess fabric beneath your applique, the applique stitches which you can see from the backside of the piece will be your guide. Snipping ¼" inside of those stitches, continue to cut parallel to them in order to cut the background

fabric away from under your applique. Then, carefully peel away your seam allowances, which have been stuck, and remove the paper. Rather than pull the paper out and away from the seam allowances, I use my nail to scrape the seam allowance away from the paper and then just lift the paper out. By scraping the fabric away, you tend to pull less on the seam allowances and loosen fewer threads. (Figure 9-7)

The discovery of this method opened up the world of applique. I no longer needed to rely on the expertise of my untrained fingers to fold those fabric edges under. The freezer paper did the work for me. If you have never done any applique and would like to give it a shot, I recommend this method. It will give you the feeling of success and the confidence to try other methods. You will have a sense of what you are trying to achieve.

METHOD FOUR – Pressing Freezer Paper To Your Fabric
- Make a template of each of your pattern pieces.
- Trace the pattern on the dull side of the freezer paper with the WRONG side of the pattern facing you.
- Cut the freezer paper out on the line.
- Press the freezer paper pattern piece on a piece of the intended fabric (dull side facing you).
- Cut into the fabric ¼" from the paper.
- Baste the pieces down on background fabric, overlapping seam allowances where necessary.
- Applique by turning fabric edges under with the needle over the edge of the freezer paper. (Figure 9-8)

Another option to this method is to baste the seam allowance over the edge of the freezer paper to reveal the finished applique piece prior to basting it down on the background fabric.

This method comes in handy when your pattern pieces are so small that the first method of freezer paper applique does not work well because there is not enough freezer paper showing to hold the seam allowances, such as in a small narrow leaf. (Figure 9-9)

Figure 9-6

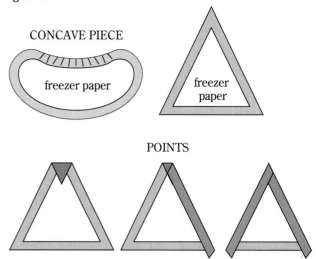

CONCAVE PIECE

freezer paper

freezer paper

POINTS

Figure 9-7

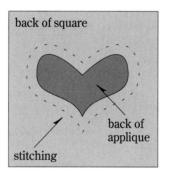

back of square

back of applique

stitching

Figure 9-8

Figure 9-9

freezer paper

Figure 9-10

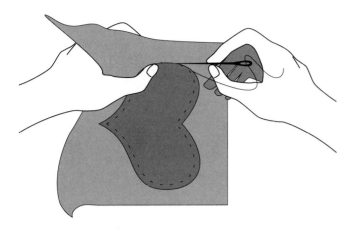

Figure 9-11

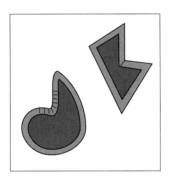

TRICK

When you come to a concave curve, put your needle at the END of the area and sweep the needle down towards your fingers to get the edge to turn under neatly.

•

When you come to a sharp inside angle, remember that at that end point there is no seam allowance to turn under. It has gone to one side or the other. Take a few very neat and close together stitches there to secure the inner point of the angle.

•

As you approach the tip of an outside pointed angle, tuck in the top seam allowance, then tuck in the seam allowance you are sewing and continue to the point and down the other side.

METHOD FIVE – Needle Turning
• Make a template of each of your different pattern pieces.
• Trace the pattern on the wrong side of your fabric with the wrong side of your template facing you.
• Cut the pattern out a scant ¼" away from the line.
• Position pieces on the background fabric and baste down ½" in from the cut edge.
• Applique the pieces down by holding the backing and applique fabric between your thumb and first finger and taking the side of your needle and pushing the edge in and pinching it until you are able to sew. Only attempt a small bit at a time and use a very slim seam allowance. (Figure 9-10)

This method is not as difficult as it sounds and actually works quite well for many novices. Like everything else, the more you do it the better you will become. Being someone who used to rely solely on the freezer paper method, I would strongly urge you to practice the needle turn method in order to gain expertise. Once you have mastered this method, it gives you the greatest amount of flexibility with the least amount of effort. You will need to clip concave curves and sharp angles. (Figure 9-11)

METHOD SIX – Starch Method
• Follow the first three steps in Method Five to prepare your fabric pieces.
• Position a posterboard template wrong side up inside the lines, and dampen the seam allowance with liquid starch.
• Using a stiletto, pull the seam allowance over the edge and press with a dry iron on the cotton setting.
• Run the stiletto under the seam allowance of the completed unit to remove the template.
• Position and baste in place.

This method works very well and a nice edge is not difficult to achieve.

BIAS STRIPS IN APPLIQUE

Sometimes strips of fabric which are appliqued need to curve. Stems for flowers and basket handles are places where bias strips are often used around curves. The easiest way to make a strip of fabric curve is to cut the fabric along the bias. (Figure 9-12)

It would be very tedious to turn under two bias edges on a very narrow strip so there are two methods you can use to accomplish this task.

METHOD ONE
• Cut your bias strip and fold it in half, wrong sides together and press. Place the raw edge over the place you would like and stitch with a running stitch, a scant ¼" through the strip into the background. (Figure 9-13)
• Fold the folded edge over the first line of sewing and applique the other side.

METHOD TWO
Another method is to stitch the two raw edges together on the sewing machine (wrong sides together) and press the strip so that the stitching and the seam allowance are hidden underneath. (Figure 9-14) Then you can position the strip on the background fabric and applique both edges.

Either of these methods can be used to applique straight strips as well.

CIRCLES

The seam allowance on circular shapes can be gathered with a running stitch around a cardboard template and pressed into position to achieve a uniform shape. Carefully remove the template and baste into place.

Figure 9-12

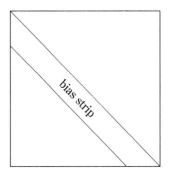

Figure 9-13

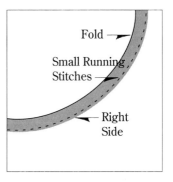

Figure 9-14

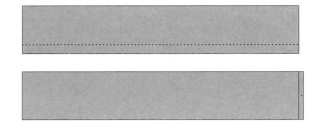

TRICK

When using Method One on a curve, whenever possible, sew the raw edges along the widest portion of the curve (convex portion) so that the fabric will stretch when the folded portion is brought over the running stitch and is appliqued.

Figure 9-15

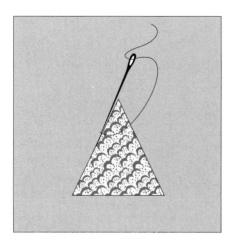

Figure 9-16

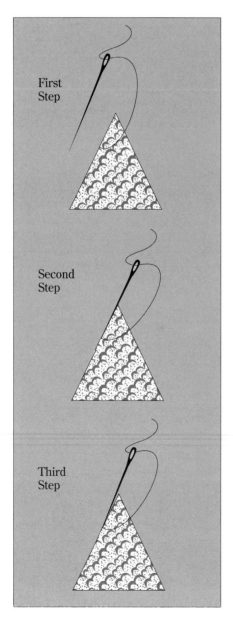

First
Step

Second
Step

Third
Step

THE APPLIQUE STITCH

The most common stitches used in applique are the blind stitch and the slip stitch. The idea is to not let your stitch be seen.

• Match thread color to top piece of fabric, using a single knotted thread.

• Thin needle.

• Cotton fabric.

• Edges prepared or not, depending on the method used.

• All the pieces positioned and anchored with basting on the background fabric.

You are now ready to applique with one of the following two stitches:

BLIND STITCH: Bring the needle with a single knotted thread up from the back and through the folded edge of the applique seam allowance, picking up only a few threads.

Insert the needle down into the background fabric *directly across* from where the thread is and travel the needle underneath a minute amount before it comes back up through the background and the edge of the applique. (Figure 9-15)

SLIP STITCH: This stitch requires that you come up from the back and instead of picking up the edge of the fold, you slip your needle into and along the fold and bring your needle out on top of your work. The needle is then inserted into the background fabric to the back of the work where you begin the process again. This stitch has three stitch motions (although step one and step two are often done in one motion), the movement from the back, into and along the fold and the movement from the top into the back of the work again. (Figure 9-16)

Make your stitches fairly tight, but not so tight that they gather the edge of the fabric.

SEWING PIECES
ON TOP OF OTHER PIECES

It is only necessary to sew through the piece of fabric immediately underneath and not all the way through to the background when you have layered pieces. This is a hard and fast rule if you plan to cut the background fabric away.

You can sew all the way through the piece to the background fabric, but be warned that you will then not be able to cut it away, as you would be cutting through your stitching.

When one piece of fabric tucks under another piece, you only need to sew up the new piece. (Figure 9-17)

SHALL I CUT AWAY
THE BACKGROUND FABRIC?

Whether or not to cut the background away from underneath your applique piece is a decision you make based upon several criteria. If you used the freezer paper, you have to cut it away, or at least slit it, in order to get the freezer paper out.

If you did not use freezer paper and only turned the fabric under with your needle, you do not have to cut the background away. Bear in mind, however, that if you plan to quilt inside the area of applique you will *want* to cut the background fabric away so that it will not be necessary for you to quilt through that extra layer or layers of fabric. Sometimes it may be necessary to cut away more than just the background fabric in order to quilt the desired area. This would be the case when one piece is layered on top of another piece. As long as you do not cut into your applique stitches, you should have no problem cutting away under layers.

Figure 9-17

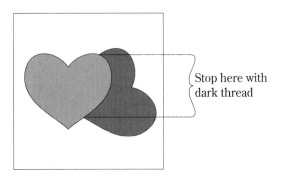

Stop here with dark thread

TRICK

ENDING THE APPLIQUE THREAD

To make a nice neat knot when ending your applique thread try the following:

• Working from the back of the block, take a backstitch into the seam allowance.

• Place the needle back into the same stitch, leaving about an inch exposed.

• Take the two threads from the eye of the needle and wrap them under the point of the needle to the right.

• Take the other end of the thread which is coming from the seam allowance area and wrap it under the point of the needle to the left.

• Pull the needle through the wraps and cut thread about one inch away.

Figure 9-18

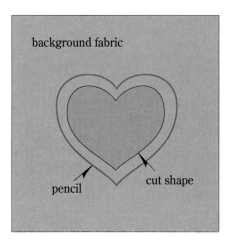

Figure 9-19

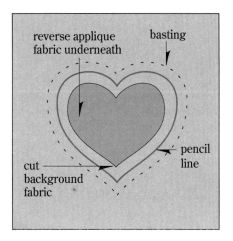

REVERSE APPLIQUE

This is a technique whereby the fabric that is going to be the design is basted UNDERNEATH the background fabric. The background fabric is lightly marked on the right side with the desired design. The background fabric is then cut away a scant ¼" inside the pencil lines. Some quilters cut away prior to basting the fabric beneath so they don't chance snipping it with their scissors and others wait until the fabric has been basted beneath. (Figure 9-18)

A piece of fabric which is slightly larger than each design area is placed underneath the background fabric in the appropriate area and basted ¼" outside the pencil line. It may be that one piece of the same fabric or several different fabrics are used beneath the piece of backing fabric. A light box is a helpful aid in making sure the fabric beneath has been placed in the correct location. (Figure 9-19)

Now, using thread which matches the BACK-GROUND fabric, the seam allowances are pushed back with the needle to the pencil markings and appliqued down with a blindstitch or slip stitch. Curves and sharp angles will need to be clipped as you work. Once the sewing is complete, the basting can be removed and any excess fabric which was basted underneath can be trimmed close to the stitching.

Traditional Applique Blocks

(Full size templates for a 12" finished block are in Appendix III.)

American Beauty Rose
(3 templates)

Bride's Quilt
(2 templates)

Butterfly
(3 templates)

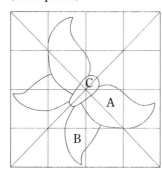

Lancaster Rose
(5 templates)

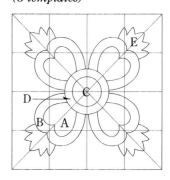

Oak Leaf & Cherries
(2 templates)

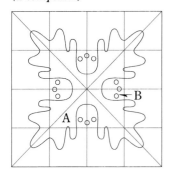

Tulip Quilt
(3 templates)

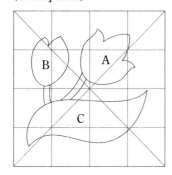

Triple Tulip
(8 templates)

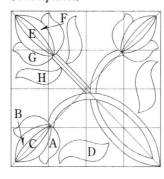

Tulip Time
(4 templates)

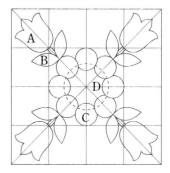

Chapter Ten

Machine Piecing

Contrary to what many may believe, the words *sewing machine* are not dirty words to most quilters. Quilters often use their sewing machine to piece part of their quilt tops, and many machine piece their entire quilt tops. Some even quilt by machine. Whether or not you should use your machine depends on several variables.

If you are very comfortable sitting at your machine and enjoy sewing on it, you should seek out machine piecing.

But if you are uncomfortable sitting at the sewing machine, you should probably do two things. First, take the time to familiarize yourself with your machine and all it can do, in order to give yourself more confidence when you do want to use it. Secondly, you should probably rely on your hand piecing when speed is not a necessity and the seams are short, and on your sewing machine when sewing long straight seams such as borders.

However, if you need a quilt in very little time, there is absolutely no way to hand piece several hundred pieces quickly. If speed is your criterion, you need your sewing machine.

If you are going to make a very simple repetitive design, the old adage, "familiarity breeds contempt," may fit. If you are the type of person who resents doing the same thing over and over again and becomes bored without a challenge, a quilt that involves many repeated units should be tackled on the sewing machine.

If you decide to piece your quilt on the sewing machine, you should use 100% cotton fabric. I don't use blends for patchwork on the sewing machine. They just don't have the body and will slip and slide.

The point that I am trying to make is that you will be the ultimate judge of whether to work on the machine or not. Probably the most important factor is *you*. How do you feel about the sewing machine? If you don't like sitting at your machine, then long tedious projects will seem like work and will be avoided. If, on the other hand, handwork seems too time consuming and you love the speed of your machine, you will seek out projects that work well for you on the machine. The idea is to do what you do best under the circumstances.

ADDING SEAM ALLOWANCES

As you have already read, the standard seam allowance for patchwork is ¼".

That means that to convert your patchwork to machine sewing, it will be necessary for you to add a ¼" seam allowance to all sides of your template and then sew seams ¼" in from the cut edge with your sewing machine. There will be no sewing line; you will rely on your sewing machine to standardize your seams, using the edge of your presser foot or a guide. It is a wonderful thought, but it doesn't always happen. Not all sewing machines needles are positioned exactly ¼" in from the edge of the presser foot or the ¼" mark on the guide. Some machines allow for the movement of the needle position whereby the perfect ¼" from the needle to the edge of the presser foot can be achieved. (Figure 10-1)

CHECKING SEWING MACHINE SEAM ALLOWANCE

First, take a clear plastic ruler which marks off inches in at least quarters and place it under your presser foot and drop your needle down so that the needle will fall *exactly* ¼" in from the edge. (Figure 10-2)

What you are checking is where ¼" falls in relation to the needle. My experience has been that for many sewing machines the ¼" mark falls just under the presser foot, which means that if you use the edge of the presser foot as your guide, your seam allowances will actually be *wider* than ¼". If this is the case, you can make the decision to use one of the following methods.

Figure 10-1

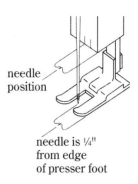

needle
position

needle is ¼"
from edge
of presser foot

Figure 10-2

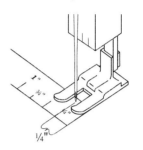

¼

Figure 10-3

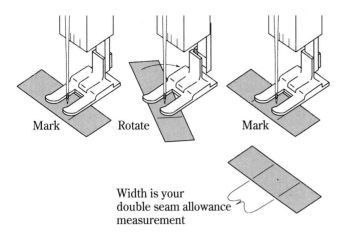

Mark   Rotate   Mark

Width is your
double seam allowance
measurement

Figure 10-4

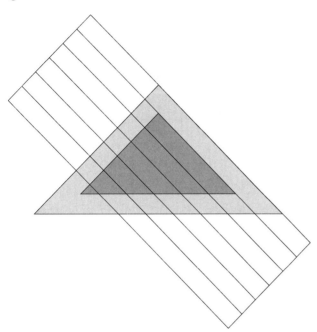

METHOD ONE

Add the correct seam allowance for your machine. You can measure your seam allowance by dropping your needle on a piece of paper and drawing a line on the edge of your presser foot. Now lift the presser foot and rotate the paper halfway around and drop the presser foot again and mark a parallel line along the edge once more. The distance between these two lines is *your* seam allowance doubled. Let's say for the sake of explanation your measurement is ⅝". If you were going to sew a finished 2" square, you would cut a 2⅝" square instead of the standard 2½" square in order to allow for *your* larger seam allowance. Now that you know what type of a seam allowance you will be sewing, you can add *your measurement* to the finished patchwork measurement. This works fine for patchwork such as squares and rectangles. (Figure 10-3)

However, triangles, rhomboids and angled patchwork require that you add the actual single seam allowance to each side of your template. This can be accomplished by placing a see-through ruler over the finished size and drawing your actual seam allowance. (Figure 10-4)

METHOD TWO

Develop measurements as you piece. You can develop sizes in relation to your seam allowance as you sew. For example, if your block consists of two seamed squares which are then pieced to a solid piece you could cut the seamed squares adding the standard ¼" to each side and sew them. Then you would measure the two-square unit, including seam allowance, to determine what size to cut the piece it will be added to. This same concept holds true for any pieced unit which will be added to another unit. (Figure 10-5)

Using this method, your pieces are cut to fit the sewn pieces; therefore, your quilt may be larger or smaller depending on the size of your machine seam allowance. (Figure 10-6)

Figure 10-5

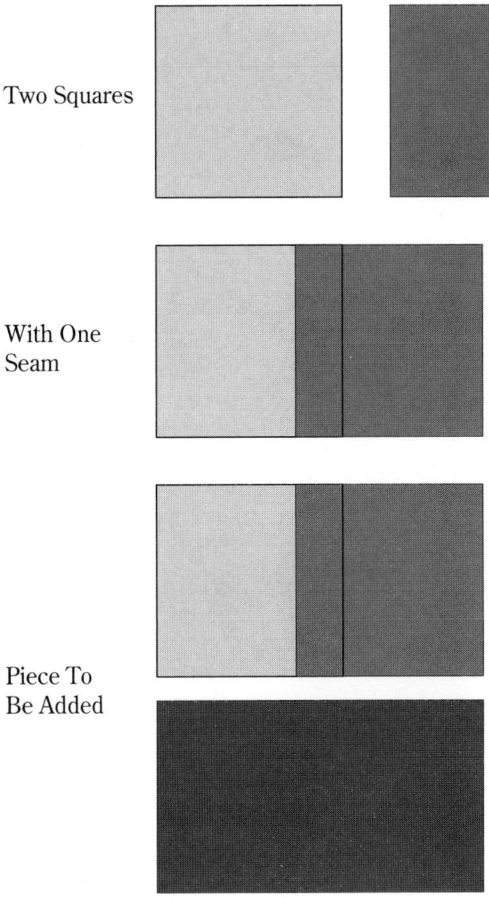

Two Squares

With One Seam

Piece To Be Added

Figure 10-6

Figure 10-7

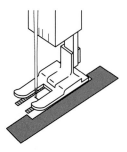

Figure 10-8

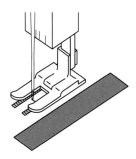

METHOD THREE

Mark the exact ¼" seam allowance on your machine even though it does not correspond with the edge of your presser foot.

The last alternative is to mark the exact ¼" seam allowance on your sewing machine even though it falls inside the presser foot or beyond the edge of the presser foot. If the exact ¼" falls inside the edge of your presser foot, you will want to notch out the tape guide under the presser foot, so the tape will not interfere with the feed dogs of the machine or the pressure of the foot on the fabric. (Figure 10-7)

If, on the other hand, the ¼" measurement from the needle falls beyond the edge of the presser foot, you can more easily accommodate by making a masking tape guide across the face plate of the machine. (Figure 10-8)

MAKING A MASKING TAPE GUIDE

Figure 10-9

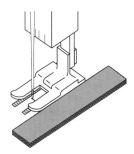

Whatever method you decide you feel most comfortable with, you will want all your seam allowances to be straight and steady. To do this, I make a masking tape guide on the sewing machine which will guide my fabric in a straight line to the needle. To make this guide, I place a length of masking tape on the sewing machine just along the presser foot, or adjust as needed, and continue the tape straight through across the back. Once you have placed one piece of tape down, add about five or six more right on top so you will have a ridge. If your sewing machine is the type that has the sewing surface which pulls off, you can slit the tape straight through with an exacto knife in order to be able to remove the surface. (Figure 10-9)

The purpose of this guide is that your fabric will feed straight through in an even fashion with a minimum amount of manipulation.

If you are using Method Three and your ¼" seam allowance mark falls under your presser foot, you can run the tape along the edge of the ruler. However, only go up to the presser foot and notch out the tape the length of your feed dogs. You cannot go over them, as they are the apparatus which pulls your fabric through as it is being sewn.

Figure 10-10

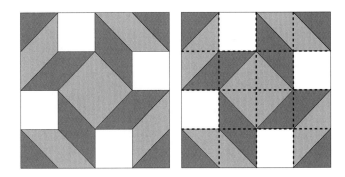

CHANGING PATCHWORK
FOR MACHINE WORK

If you have determined that the block you are going to piece is going to be pieced on the sewing machine, you may want to add seams in order to piece the block in straight line units. (Figure 10-10)

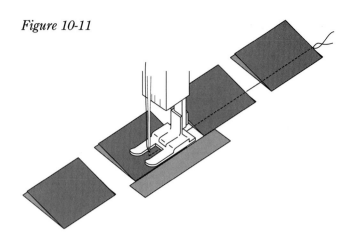

Figure 10-11

SPEED SEWING

There are several things you can do to speed up piecing at the sewing machine.

• Have a fast state of mind. Sew as quickly as you can and still manipulate the fabric correctly. Don't plod along at the speed of a waltz when the jitterbug will yield the same results.

• Continuous feeding. If you have a repetitive seam to sew, such as one blue square getting sewn to one red square continuously feed those two squares into the sewing machine without cutting the thread. (Figure 10-11)

Figure 10-12

6" Block

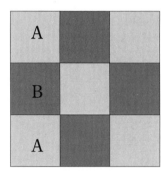

STRIP, STRIP, STRIP

So much can be done with strips of fabric cut with the rotary cutter and grid ruler.

For example, if you need to make a nine patch using the combination in Figure 10-12, you would cut two strips of fabric using fabric A and one strip of fabric using fabric B. Your first combination would be a strip of fabric A, a strip of fabric B and another strip of fabric A. (Figure 10-13) Your second combination would be just the reverse.(Figure 10-14)

Figure 10-13

Sizes after sewn

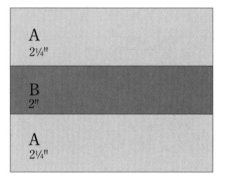

Figure 10-14

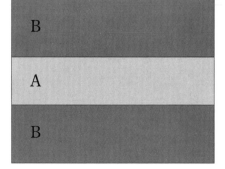

Once you have sewn these two separate pieces together, you will want to take them over to the ironing board and press the seam allowances in one direction. The allowances should be pressed in the same direction unless you would be able to see the allowance through a lighter fabric in which case you would press to the dark side.

Now, using your rotary cutter and grided ruler, cut these sewn strips apart at the same width that you cut the strips. You now have two stacks of different combinations. (Figure 10-15)

Take one piece from the first stack, place it right side up, put one piece from the second stack on top, and seam these with the seam allowances going in opposite directions. The seam allowances going in opposite directions help to lock the pieces into position to be sewn together, giving better alignment where the seams cross. (Figure 10-16)

Now it may happen along the way that on one piece the seam allowance goes in both directions. If this does happen, just press it flat. (Figure 10-17)

Figure 10-15

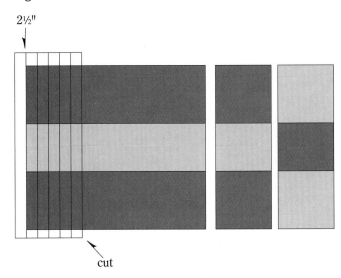

2½"

cut

Figure 10-16

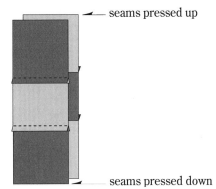

seams pressed up

seams pressed down

Figure 10-17

Seam allowances pressed in both directions because of light fabric.

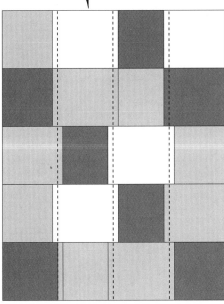

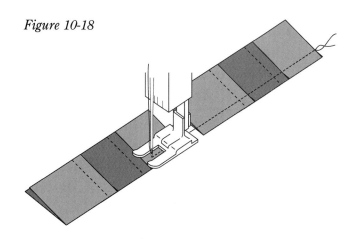

Figure 10-18

Once you have sewn one set together, *do not take it out of the machine*, but continue to feed as many sets through as needed. (Figure 10-18)

Another alternative to adding pieces through continuously, is adding pieced pieces to a solid strip. (Figure 10-19)

Once the seam is sewn, the units can be cut apart exactly at the correct size.(Figure 10-20)

Figure 10-19

Figure 10-20

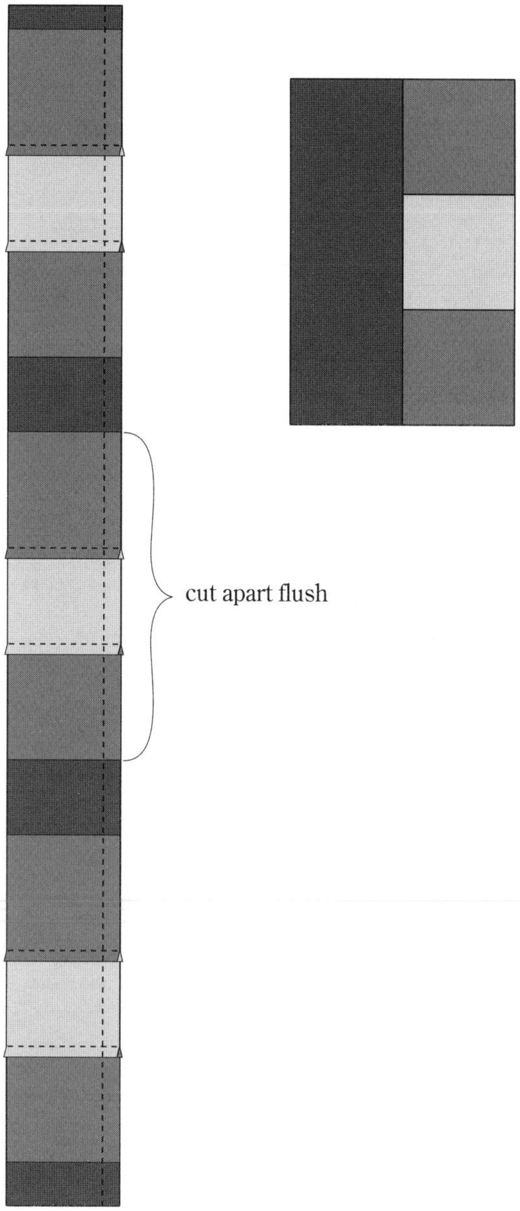

cut apart flush

These are just a few tips for a basis for quick machine work. There are several books out on the market which go into great detail explaining the mechanics of quick strip piecing, quick triangle piecing, etc. which will make your machine work for you. There are many quilts which can be worked up beautifully on the sewing machine. Not all the quilts you make need to be a long time investment. You are allowed to make quick quilts. Using quick methods, you can make many quilts and give them away to others freely, pleasing both yourself and others.

I have often joked with friends that I have hand pieced and hand quilted original Medallion quilts for both my young sons when they get married, should they marry the *right* woman. This statement almost always evokes a chuckle from quilters. I know their laughter is an acknowledgment that a year's worth of handwork should be given to someone special who will appreciate and care for it.

My sons will both be presented with quilts upon the occasion of their marriage, but the quilts may be tied, machine-pieced quilts given with much love and no regrets.

Chapter Eleven

Top Construction, Design Marking, Sandwiching & Basting

PUTTING YOUR QUILT TOGETHER

Thus far we have discussed everything concerned with putting a unit or block together. Now we need to talk about putting all of the units together in order to construct the quilt top.

BLOCK-TO-BLOCK TOPS: After you have pieced your blocks together and pressed your seam allowances, sew one block to another to make a row and then sew one row to another to make the quilt. Take care that your seam intersections meet nicely. (Figure 11-1)

Figure 11-1

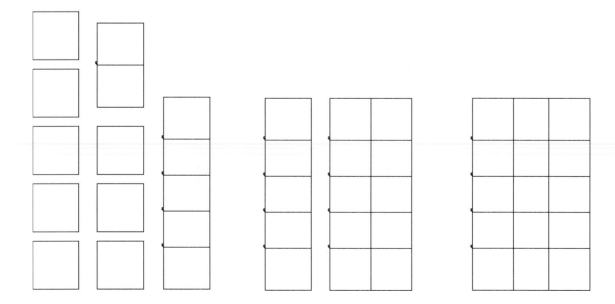

BLOCK AND SASHING TOPS: You will have a little more flexibility with this type of setting, in the event your blocks do not all turn out to be the size you intended. Make your sashing strips for the top and bottom of each block including seam allowances. Mark the sewing lines on the sashings and pin your pieced block to the top and bottom and stretch or ease your block to fit the sashing. (Figure 11-2)

Now make your lengthwise strips the size the block is supposed to be, plus the width of the top sashing and the bottom sashing, plus ½" seam allowance. For instance, a 3" sashing around a 12" block would be cut 3½" x 12½" for the top and bottom and 3½" x 18½" for each side. (Figure 11-3)

If you are setting together several rows with sashing, you would first connect all the blocks with top and bottom strips for your vertical rows. Your lengthwise strip would be marked at each interval to indicate the beginning and ending points of each block and intersecting sashings. (Figure 11-4)

Figure 11-3

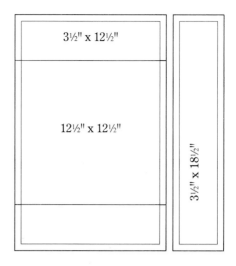

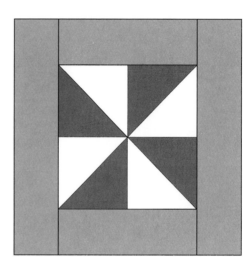

Figure 11-2

Back

Front

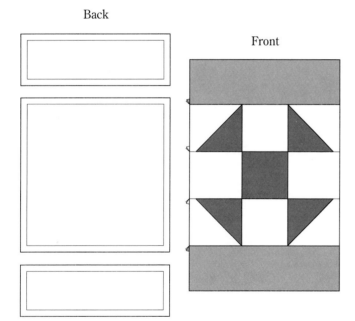

Figure 11-4

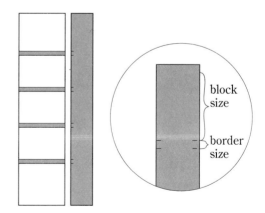

Figure 11-5

12" finished/12½" unfinished

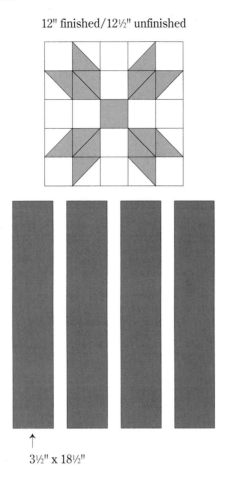

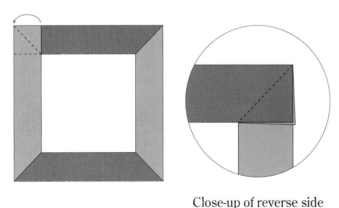

3½" x 18½"

MITERED CORNERS: You may decide to miter corners (seam them at a 45° angle) in your borders. To do this you must be sure to make all your borders the length necessary for the side of the quilt or quilt block you are bordering PLUS the width of each border it crosses and seam allowance. This means all four strips would be the same length and width if you were bordering a square. A 12" square with a 3" border would need four strips cut 3½" wide by 18½" long. (Figure 11-5)

One of the easiest methods I have found to miter a corner is to sew each strip to the block (again easing or stretching the block to fit the size it is intended to be) and stop at the finished corner point. Lay one strip out flat and take the other strip and, placing it on top, fold it back on itself at a 45° angle and lightly press with the iron. Be careful not to drag the iron across the bias of the fabric. Pin the fold in place and applique down. Once sewn, trim away the excess. (Figure 11-6)

To machine or hand piece the mitered corner, mark your 45° angle on the wrong side of both sashings, pin the lines together so they coincide and then piece by hand or on the machine along the matching lines. Trim away the excess once the seam has been sewn. Press both seam allowances to one side. (Figure 11-7)

Figure 11-6

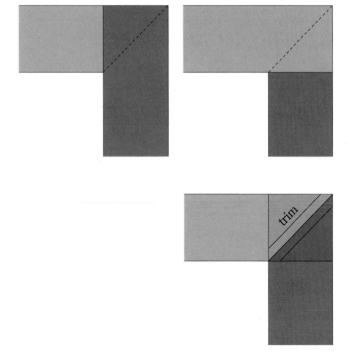

Close-up of reverse side

Figure 11-7

MEDALLION-STYLE QUILTS: This type of central focus quilt is usually pieced from the center to the perimeter. The area which you need to be careful of here is your dimensions. It is easy for your piecing to make your top grow or shrink in size. Since the quilt is planned on the basis of inches, you need to constantly check the dimensions of your quilt top and make sure that sections which have grown are eased in to fit. You do have some flexibility here as a small amount of fullness should work out in your quilting, but you don't want to end up with the battle of the bulge. As long as you use your ruler often, you can keep this type of a problem in check.

MEASURING AND SEWING LONG BORDERS: When measuring your finished piecework to add long borders, always measure through the middle of each side rather than along the edge. If necessary, ease the outside edge to fit this measurement when adding the border. If you are sewing your quilt together totally by hand and want to call it a hand pieced quilt, you will want to sew them on by hand.

If you are sewing your quilt together totally by hand and don't care whether it carries the "totally hand pieced" label, then by all means use the sewing machine. When sewing borders on by machine, mark the ends and the middle and pin them completely on before sewing. Don't just take the necessary size border and begin sewing it on by machine and expect it to fit. The sewing machine can stretch or ease the fabric depending upon how you are feeding the fabric.

DECIDING WHEN TO MARK THE QUILTING DESIGN

Once the quilt is entirely assembled, you can now mark the quilting designs *or* you may proceed to layering the top with the batting and the backing (sandwiching) and baste the quilt. The marking of the quilting designs can be done before or after the quilt is sandwiched, just so long as you are *not* relying on seeing through the fabric to trace your quilting design. If you are relying upon this "see-through" method described later in this chapter, then you must put these markings on prior to sandwiching the quilt. If both options are open, the before or after question usually comes down to preference. Some quilters feel marking the quilt all at once is tedious and prefer to mark as they quilt and others prefer to mark on just the one layer and would rather mark the quilt all at once. Continuous border designs which need to meet in a certain place do need to be marked all at once so they will meet. Other areas which are marked individually can be marked as they are being quilted or all at once.

Figure 11-8

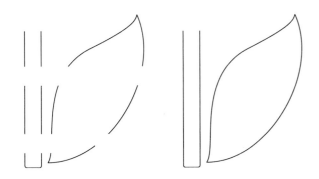

USING STENCILS

These are usually plastic and cardboard pieces which have a design cut out of them and are used to mark the quilt top.

Stencils come in many sizes and many, many designs. Remember, too, that you can combine stencils, use only portions of them and use them across seam lines. They are just another tool for you to use in your own way. The cut out lines are not continuous because the stencil would fall apart if they were. There will often be "hedges" across the quilt line. Remember when quilting that you connect the lines broken by these. (Figure 11-8)

MARKING A QUILTING DESIGN

When using a stencil or marking any line on the top of the quilt there are several products out on the market you can use.

LEAD PENCILS: If you are going to mark with a lead pencil, use a No. 4, hard lead pencil. These can be purchased in quilt shops, business supply stores, art stores and some stationery stores. Do not use a No. 2 lead pencil as it is so soft that the lines may smudge, the markings will be too dark and the color of the lead will be picked up by your quilting thread. Do not make the line on the quilt any darker than is necessary for you to see. The pencil will not wash out, so you want to mark so lightly that the shadow created by the line of quilting will make it appear that the pencil line is not there.

White, yellow or silver pencils, and standard colored pencils in various brands are often used on very dark or busy fabrics where a lead pencil is not visible.

CHALK MARKERS: There are several types including pencils and wheels, which place chalk lines. They work fine but you won't want to mark more than you are ready to quilt at any one time, as the chalk will rub off easily.

DISAPPEARING AND WASHOUT MARKERS: There are several products on the market which make these types of claims. They appeared to be very innovative when first introduced several years ago. Now, because of several bad experiences, such as their reappearing in humid conditions and because of unknown possible future effects on the fabric, many feel they are not a preferred way to mark a quilt.

CINNAMON AND CORNSTARCH: When I first became involved with quilting, I was told, as I am sure many others were told, that pioneer women used to make needle holes in paper designs and then rub cornstarch or cinnamon over them, depending on the color of the fabric being marked. I was recently told, while taking a workshop on old quilts, that such a practice probably was not the case as both those substances would have attracted far too many insects to the quilt. Another piece of folklore, crushed.

MASKING TAPE: Anytime you need to quilt a straight line, you can use a piece of masking tape on the top of the quilt as a guide to quilt along. Once you have quilted that area, the masking tape can be moved and reused several times. If the tape I am using is really sticky, I like to dab it on a piece of furniture where it might pick up a little lint and lose some of its stickiness. If it is too sticky, it is liable to start pulling the batting through the fabric and start some fiber migration (or bearding) that I would just as soon not have. If I am quilting on a solid dark fabric, I prefer to mark the straight lines with a pencil and not risk the migration. Laying ¼" masking tape along a seam line that you would like to outline quilt is, though, a boon to the new quilter who is having difficulty estimating a ¼" distance. Hopefully, once you have become familiar with the ¼" you will be able to discard your masking tape in order to speed up the process of quilting. If you do use tape, be careful not to run your quilting needle into the edge of the tape, as it will gum up your needle and make quilting more difficult.

LIGHT BOX USE FOR MARKING THE TOP: Sometimes the quilting design that you want to use is not a stencil but rather it is a drawing and you need to trace the design by seeing through the fabric. A solid black line drawing can easily be seen through most very light fabrics. If a fabric is too dark for you to see the design through, you will want to use a light box. This entire process will need to be taken care of prior to sandwiching and basting the quilt. Use of a light box was more fully explained in the chapter on applique.

LAYING ON: The technique of "laying on" is one other way to mark your top. With this method, the needle that you are quilting with is drawn across the fabric around a shape or along a straight edge in order to mark the fabric. This works well when done just before you are going to quilt the area. This type of marking does not work well with very intricate designs because the markings are very faint.

MARKING BY MAKING A CREASE: A stainless steel butter knife that does not have a serrated edge can be used very effectively to make straight lines or slightly curved lines on your quilt top by making a crease in the fabric. A hera, a plastic tool developed by the Japanese, can also be used to make crease lines for quilting. This method is most effective on solid fabrics or fabrics which are not too busy. Background grid lines or lines marked uniformly from seam lines with a ruler allow for uniform quilting. These lines will stay for quite some time so this procedure can be used prior to sandwiching the quilt top or after the quilt is sandwiched. As with any method, you should test the tool you will be using on a similar piece of fabric to assure that it will not damage your fabric and that you will be able to see these lines on your particular fabric.

Figure 11-9

Figure 11-10

Figure 11-11

SOME TRADITIONAL TYPES OF QUILTING DESIGNS

OUTLINE QUILTING: Quilting ¼" away from a seam line. You may decide to outline quilt around some of the patches or you may want to outline quilt around all of the patches. Quilt just outside the seam allowance so you will be quilting through the top, batting and backing only. A nice even seam allowance on your patches will help you make your outline quilting uniform. (Figure 11-9)

IN-THE-DITCH QUILTING: Quilting "in the ditch" is quilting right next to the seam line on the fabric piece which does not have the seam allowance under it. This side is called the "down side." You can tell which side has the seam allowances and is not the "down side" by looking along the seam line to see which side looks flatter or lower than the other. The advantage of quilting "in the ditch" is that the quilting stitch is very difficult to see. But, the disadvantage is that you are constantly working along the seam allowances where you are manipulating several layers. This does become tiring on the fingers. (Figure 11-10)

ECHO QUILTING: Quilting around a shape (usually done in conjunction with applique) in successive and more casual lines. (Figure 11-11)

STIPPLE QUILTING: Stipple Quilting is quilting which is done either like echo quilting or in a meandering fashion, in very close lines (1/16" to 1/8" apart). Stipple quilting requires many stitches and very often stretches out the area you are quilting, distorting the fabric. Before you decide to stipple your piece, try a sample. (Figure 11-12)

BACKGROUND QUILTING: Quilting which is done to fill in the entire background of an area. The more common types used are grids and clamshells. (Figure 11-13)

Figure 11-12

Figure 11-13

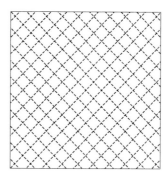

TRICK

When using a grid for background quilting, place your lines diagonally to coincide with the bias of the quilt. The fabric will have more flexibility and your straight lines will be easier to quilt. (Figure 11-14)

Figure 11-14

This

Not This

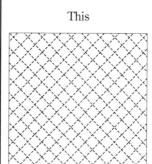
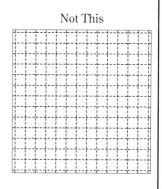

Figure 11-15

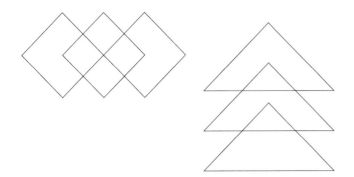

PLANNING QUILTING DESIGNS FOR A QUILT

First and foremost, don't spend a great deal of time marking and quilting a beautiful design on a portion of the quilt where it will not show up because of intricate piecing or busy fabric. Those areas should be outline quilted or quilted with large designs which will show up. Save the intricate designs for mini-prints, solids and open areas.

When still in the planning stages, choose some fabrics which will allow quilting to be featured and save some areas in your quilt for quilting.

You can use themes like hearts, flowers, cables, interlocking geometric shapes and feathered designs in your quilt. Often, just a part of a stencil can be used in an area where the entire stencil cannot be accommodated.

Sometimes you can make interesting designs by just interlocking a simple graphic shape. (Figure 11-15)

The quilting design can have a great effect on your quilt's design. If you quilt around something, it will appear to raise up. You can soften angles by using curves in your quilting.

Set realistic goals when deciding how to quilt the top. Decide approximately how long it will take you to quilt what you have intended. If you have a 12-block quilt and you have decided that you can probably quilt one block a day and the border you have chosen to quilt will probably take you three days for each side, that is a total of 24 days. (When I say day, I am referring to the time you feel you can put aside to quilt this quilt each day or evening, not 24 hours). As presumed, the quilt will involve approximately a month's commitment. Is that the type of commitment you had in mind for quilting this quilt? If so, begin and make any decisions about adding more quilting when you are finished. You may feel the quilt needs more, and that you are willing to put more time in or you may feel the quilt looks just fine and you are ready to bind it. There is some flexibility.

Look at antique quilts, quilt shows, quilt books to find new ideas of what and where to quilt. I always go to quilt shows with a camera and/or notebook to take pictures of quilts, not so much because I plan to go and make that quilt, but because perhaps a color scheme or an unusual quilting arrangement may catch my eye.

MARKING BORDERS SO THE QUILTING DESIGN MEETS ACCURATELY IN THE CORNERS

Use your stencil and mark the corner sections of the border first. Place the straight part of the design along the border and judge how close your design will come to naturally falling in place for the next corner to match up. If your design ends short of the corner, lengthen each section just a fraction and if you are long, shorten each section a fraction. Keep checking your progress as you mark so you can adjust accordingly. (Figure 11-16)

If your stencil did not come with a corner unit, experiment first on a piece of paper to develop a corner that you will be happy with using parts of your design. (Figure 11-17)

Figure 11-16

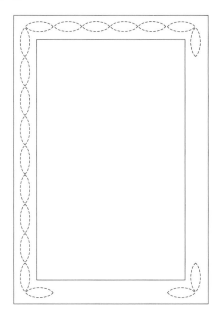

Figure 11-17

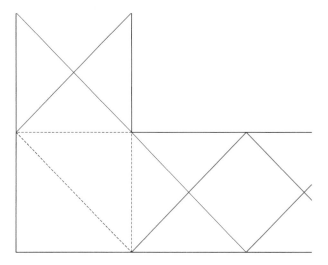

Figure 11-18

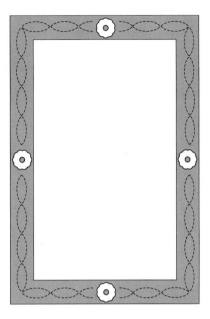

You can mark from the corners towards the center of each side and just have them meet in an alternate quilted unit or pieced unit instead of being continuous. (Figure 11-18)

You also can eliminate the corner turn completely by placing a different quilted stencil unit or a pieced unit in the corners. (Figure 11-19)

Figure 11-19

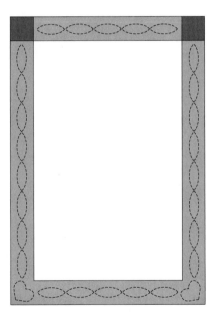

SANDWICH AND BASTE

When the top of your quilt is complete, it is time for you to sandwich and baste. You will be making a sandwich of the top, a middle layer of batting and then a backing. Before we get to the actual basting process a discussion of each of these layers is helpful.

THE TOP

The top can be patchwork or applique work. It can even be one whole piece of cloth which is only going to be embellished by the quilting stitches.

A patchwork top needs to be all prepared before you are ready to baste. Make sure that all the seams have been pressed toward the darker side of the patchwork. If the fabric colors are medium to dark and there is no chance of seeing the seam allowance through, then I press to the most convenient side so as to allow the patchwork to lie flat. It is important when making your choice that you are consistent in your pressing. If you have any overlapping points which stick out, they may be clipped flush with the seam allowance. This is especially true when you have several points coming together at one place.

Make sure that any loose threads have been picked off the back. I like to use one a masking tape lint roller for this step. You will be amazed how many threads are left behind. This step is not quite so crucial with a dark or medium quilt, but many light fabrics will allow that left-behind thread to show through to the top.

An applique top needs the same attention as the patchwork top in any seamed areas; however, the appliqued portion needs attention also. Be sure that the area behind the applique has been cut away if you intend to quilt on top of the appliqued piece. If you were quilting veins inside a leaf area, you would want to cut the background fabric away behind the leaf so that you will have only one layer to quilt through.

BATTINGS

There are several types of battings available today, and new battings are often introduced to the modern quilter. Early quilters relied upon 100% cotton battings for most of their quilts, which is why most early quilts are heavily quilted and thin.

TRADITIONAL COTTON BATTINGS: This is the quilt batting generally used by quilters of long ago. If you use this type of batting, it is *important* for you to know that you must quilt about every ¼" to ½" of area. Quilts of long ago were often quilted with all-over designs of cross hatch or clamshell. This close quilting was necessary to prevent the cotton from going back into its natural form, the bole. Some of the newer cotton battings do not require quilting quite as closely as the traditional cotton batting. The batting label should indicate how closely the batting should be quilted.

COTTON/POLYESTER BATTINGS: Some battings are a combination of cotton and polyester. These blends vary in the amount of quilting recommended. It is best to check the label on the batting as to the amount of quilting needed and any other special handling required.

Generally, cotton and cotton/polyester blend battings are more difficult to quilt; however, for those who want to make the commitment, the end result is satisfying.

POLYESTER BATTINGS: The advent of polyester battings has allowed a quilter to do much less quilting on a quilt top and still have the finished quilt quite functional.

BONDED BATTINGS: Bonding means that a protective substance is placed on both sides of the batting in order to inhibit the fibers from breaking out and migrating their way through to the top of the quilt, or bearding. The cause of bearding has been discussed for several years. I believe that it has become the consensus of most quilters that the friction across the top of the quilt in constant wear will create a static charge which directs the fibers to lay in one direction and eventually work their way up through the weave of the fabric. Very dark (black and navy, etc.) solid fabrics will allow these fibers to be seen much more readily than printed fabric. You may have the same amount of bearding on lighter fabrics, but you will notice it more on these fabrics.

The following steps will reduce bearding:.
• Choose a bonded batting.
• Choose fabric with a good thread count so the fibers have to work hard in order to weave their way through to the top.
• While quilting, cover any exposed batting along the edge by overlapping your backing from the back to the front and basting it down. By covering the edge, not only do you reduce the temptation of the cat to pull at the exposed batting, prevent the batting from dusting your furniture, and keep it from snagging and being pulled apart, but you also cut down on the amount of fibers which will end up on the top of the quilt.
• If you should see bearding begin on your quilt, don't pull the fibers. You will only bring more through right behind.

TYPES OF POLYESTER BATTING: There are several thicknesses of polyester battings out on the market today, some of which are bonded and some of which are not. The packaging will tell you its size, its fiber content (cotton, polyester, etc.) and whether or not it is bonded. I will discuss each one giving you only my experiences with each. I would highly recommend that you try quilting through the batting you are considering using, before you begin a queen size quilt and discover that you are unhappy with its properties. The majority of polyester battings should be quilted every 3" to 4" or closer.
• Low Loft and Thin Batts: These types of batting are very thin battings which are very easy to quilt through. Quilts made with these will have a very thin look, much like the old quilts, and will be very lightweight. These battings are often bonded.
• Traditional: This is a fairly thin batting which allows easy quilting and gives the look of most traditional quilts. Some traditional battings are not bonded and have the density of a non-woven blanket. Traditional battings are easy to quilt.
• Extra Loft: These are battings which are thicker or fluffier than traditional battings. Some are bonded and some are not. Your quilt will have a slightly thicker look, but you may find that it is not as easy to make tiny quilting stitches through this thicker batting. These are not wrong, only different. If you wish to make a quilt which displays the tiniest quilting stitches you can make, then reconsider the low loft or traditional. If, on the other hand, you want a little thicker quilt, then you may want to consider one of the thicker battings.

• Fat Battings: Some of these thick batts are designed for quilts which are tied and not quilted. The package should indicate what the batting is designed for, quilted and/or tied quilts. If you will be tying the quilt rather than quilting it, you may want to use one of the thicker battings to give it a comforter look.

WOOL BATTING: Wool batting has a wonderful feel. It is quite a bit more expensive than polyester battings. Quilting through wool is, in my estimation, similar to quilting through an extra loft batting in thickness but needles glide very smoothly through the fibers. Wool batting can be steamed and stretched to make it a little thinner. Wool batting is not bonded, so the incidence of bearding is a factor. Most quilters who use wool batts suggest that you sandwich the batt between two layers of cheesecloth to prevent the fibers from migrating.

BATTING COLORS: The majority of battings are white or cream colored. At least one company is currently marketing a gray polyester batting for dark-colored quilts.
Some of the cotton and polyester battings still contains quite a few seed remnants, and therefore you might not want to use this type of batting in a very light quilt, where these seed remnants might be visible through the fabric.
There is one other consideration regarding color. Cotton battings do not let as much light through as the polyester battings, and therefore, an all-white quilt will have a denser white color when a white cotton batting is used.

Most of the batting companies have product information sheets available to explain the properties of each of their battings. You might want to write them or talk with your local quilt shop owner and ask for this information so you will have it as a reference as to what is currently available.
It is probably not feasible to purchase one bed size batt of each type just to try it, but you are strongly urged to quilt on the batting you have chosen before you baste an entire quilt. Just cut a small strip off an excess side or end and give it a try. If you find it is to your liking, then go ahead. If it is not, determine what it is that you are unhappy with, too thick, too thin, etc. and go from there.

PREPARING BATTING

You have made the decision which batting to use and you have brought it home from the store in its plastic bag. Most battings are sold in crib, full, queen and king size. Some stores do sell batting by the yard off a large roll also. Obviously, if you are making a couple of pillows or a small project, then the quantity off the roll may be just what you need.

The day before you are ready to sandwich your quilt, you want to take the batting out of the bag and allow it to unroll and lose its curl. It will be easier to handle if you give it this time. It can also be put in the electric or gas dryer, on air only, to allow it to relax.

SEAMING BATTING

If your project is larger than the piece of batting you have, you can seam your battings by laying one next to the other and stitching them together. Your goal is to not have any gaps or heavy ridges, but to have a smooth surface when you run your hand over it. (Figure 11-20)

QUILT BACKINGS

SIZE: The backing and batting should be larger than the top to allow for shrinkage during the quilting process. A couple of inches all around is sufficient. The backing is the last layer of the sandwich. You can purchase bleached and unbleached muslin 90" wide which can be used as the backing of a quilt. You can purchase cotton fabric 45" wide, cut off both selvages from the seaming edges and make one seam up the middle in order to have a scant 90" backing.

You can purchase cotton fabric 45" wide and add the other 45" by adding two pieces and making two seams down the back. Again, don't forget to cut off the selvages along the edges that are being sewn. Once the one or two seams have been sewn, press them open. You can also seam three widths of fabric together if you require a width larger than 90". (Figure 11-21)

I had made at least a dozen quilts with one seam in the back before I found out the preferred method is to put two seams in the back.

Figure 11-20

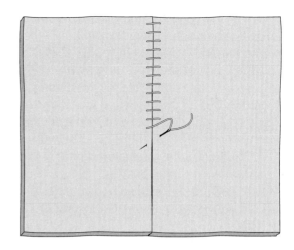

Figure 11-21

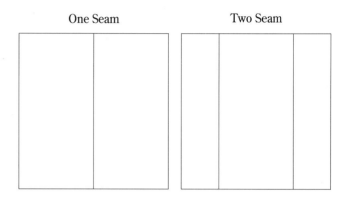

One Seam   Two Seam

Three Widths

The fabric used on the back of the quilt should complement the front. I have used solid pastels which really show off the quilting. I have also used small, one-color prints which don't allow the quilting to be seen quite so much and I have used multi-colored busier fabrics which did not allow the quilting to show much at all. There is a time and place for everything. If you plan to quilt beautiful designs with one color thread, I would use a solid fabric in white, off-white or whatever color would blend nicely with the top. You will want to show off that quilting. If you have a quilt that is going to have some nice quilting, but this is your first project and you are not quite sure how good your quilting will be, I would select a small, one-color mini-print. The quilting will show up but each little stitch will not.

If you have a quilt that you are going to quilt with several color threads and the quilting will be more to accentuate the patchwork or applique, use a multi-colored backing so the change in quilting threads will not show up and the quilting will be seen, but in a subdued way through the printed fabric.

BASTING

- The top is prepared.
- The batting has been chosen and has been taken out of the bag to uncurl.
- The backing fabric has been chosen and the necessary seam or seams have been sewn and pressed open. *(Don't forget that the backing fabric needed to be preshrunk in the washing machine and dryer).*
- Basting thread. This is simply a large spool of inexpensive white thread. You can use any sewing thread you have on hand except for very dark threads on a very light quilt. (The dye sometimes runs or leaves a residue so avoid using it for basting light quilts.)
- Large needles. I like to use size 7 cotton darners. They are nice, long, thin needles and work great for going through all three thicknesses. Some quilters like to use curved needles for basting.

Your equipment is ready, now you need the location to baste this quilt. The first quilt I basted was done on my kitchen floor. I moved all the furniture out and washed the floor very well. I then placed the three layers down, taping the backing to the floor so it would not move. Then I added the backing and top. I stretched and moved around that quilt the better part of four hours trying to baste it just right. By the time this quilt had been basted, I couldn't walk like a normal person and was sure I was in more pain than I was when I had gone through the President's physical fitness program in high school. There had to be a better way.

The easiest way is to put the tea kettle on and call one or two other quilters to come over and help you baste. When laying those three layers out smooth so they will not move, another few sets of hands cannot be prized too highly. If you are living too far from civilization to gather some extra hands, you will need to do it alone, so go slow and easy.

The following process can be done on the floor, carpeted or not, or across a large table where you can allow several inches of the edges to fall off.

- Lay the backing fabric out wrong side up and smooth it out so there are no wrinkles.
- Lay the batting on top of the backing, disturbing it as little as possible. This is where those extra hands are wonderful. They can help you hold the batting above the backing and just allow it to float down on the backing, centered, without disturbing the backing at all. Once the batting is in place you can pull the backing only toward you as the other set of hands can counter pull, making sure that the back is still flat.

• Place the top down on the batting in the same fashion as the batting was placed. Again, if you have the extra hands, allow the top to just float down centered on the batting. If you are alone, fold the top in quarters, right sides together, so that the seams are exposed and lay the quartered top down on the batting so that it is centered in one quarter of the area. (Figure 11-22)

Once it is centered you can open it in half and make sure it is still centered on one half of the quilt and then proceed to open it up all the way. Once the top is placed, smooth it out to the edges. Again, if those extra hands are still there, you can smooth from the center out to your edges as the person opposite you does the same thing at the same time. This will leave the top nice and smooth and flat.

• Thread your basting needle with a long single thread and beginning in the middle and using only one half of the thread, baste out to the outside edge. Go back and re-thread your needle with the same thread and baste off in the opposite direction to the edge. I use the following stitch to baste a quilt. (Figure 11-23)

Figure 11-22

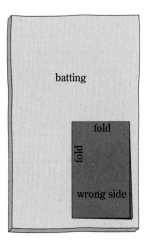

Figure 11-23

Figure 11-24

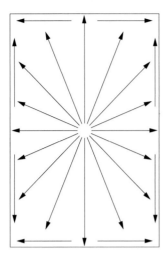

Remember to baste from the center to the outside edge and from the middle to the outside edge to the corners. *Do not baste from the corners in.* (Figure 11-24)

You can also baste in a grid-like fashion from the center out. (Figure 11-25)

This basting process will insure that the three layers will lay smooth and flat until you are ready to quilt. Do not, in your excitement, toss a basted quilt around or you will lose all that you have worked for. Always fold the quilt or roll it and unfold or unroll.

The last step when the basting is done, is to bring the excess backing fabric from the back around to the front and baste it over the exposed batting along the edge. This will eliminate so many headaches and this little bit of time will be well spent.

Your project is basted and you are now ready to quilt.

Figure 11-25

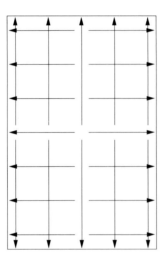

Chapter Twelve

Quilting

When I teach a seven week basic quilting class, my eager students anxiously ask, "But when are we going to quilt?" The quilting instruction takes place during the next to last week. By the time students actually have the chance to try their hand at quilting, they have invested much time and energy in fabric selection, pattern selection, and piecing, so the motivation to learn to quilt is tremendous. If I had shown them how to quilt during their first class, fifty percent of them would have said, "This is not for me," and would have ridden off into the sunset to learn how to knit. I speak from firsthand experience, because those were the exact words I uttered when I first tried my hand at quilting.

For most people, quilting feels very awkward at first – it's not unlike first learning to ride a two-wheeler. You know people do it and they say they enjoy it, but you can't seem to get the hang of it. Here's where motivation comes in. You wanted to ride the two wheeler because everyone else on the block did, so you kept at it until you were able to do it, and later you actually enjoyed it and became quite good at it.

After you have pieced or appliqued an entire quilt top, you will have the motivation you need to encourage you to continue to learn to quilt. Students I have taught to quilt have all become quilters by the time they finished quilting their first quilts. All of them could see the improvement in their stitches and began to feel the relaxing rhythm associated with quilting. Quilting had become an enjoyable task. Just keep telling yourself that if you keep quilting, you will make better stitches and you will enjoy it.

Quilting stitches bring a quilt top to life. The top, all pressed and ready to be quilted, looks flat and one dimensional. As you begin to quilt and accentuate the piecework or applique or bring new subtle design features to the top through quilting stitches, you will be further motivated to continue. The quilting adds much in the way of texture.

Before we actually get into the details of quilting, it is important to look at some of the supplies you can use. Probably, because quilting does seem awkward at first, there are many tools and supplies available.

QUILTING NEEDLES

Quilting needles are called "betweens." The sizes used by most quilters range from a size 8 to a size 12. The size 8 is the largest needle and the size 12 is the smallest. A quilting needle is shorter than a "sharp" so that it won't bend when being pushed through the layers.

If you are a beginner, I would suggest that you start with a size 9 and graduate to the smaller sizes as you become more proficient. It is not important to have the smallest stitches, but it is important for your stitches to be straight and uniform in size. If you begin to quilt with the goal of making your stitches neat and uniform, the ability to manipulate the size of your stitch will follow. If, however, your goal is to make tiny stitches, nine times out of ten, your stitches will not have that uniformity. Any quilt judge will tell you that neat and uniform stitches are far more important than tiny stitches which vary in size.

QUILTING THREAD

Quilting thread is a heavier thread than sewing thread and often is coated so that it will not fray as it is being pulled through the layers of fabric. You may quilt with sewing thread if you coat it first with beeswax which can be purchased for this purpose.

There is cotton quilting thread and cotton covered polyester quilting thread. Which one you quilt with is strictly personal preference. Some quilters use only cotton, some use cotton covered polyester and some use both. My experience with both is that I like the way the cotton thread lays on the top of cotton fabric, but if I get ambitious and try to quilt with too long a piece, the cotton thread tends to break. On the other hand, the cotton covered polyester thread, while it will not break as readily, tends to twist and form little loop knots, which need to be pulled out. Those are my experiences. You may have others. My advice is to try both kinds and use your preference when possible.

QUILTING THREAD COLORS

Quilting thread comes in many colors. The traditional color to quilt most patchwork is white or off-white. Amish quilts were traditionally quilted in black thread. When deciding what color thread to use, keep in mind a few thoughts. If you use a contrasting thread on solid fabric, each stitch you take and its length will be noticeable. Busy calicos do not let the stitches of contrasting color thread show, so fabric selection can help make stitches less noticeable, but my advice to beginners is to use a color thread which will blend with your fabric until your stitches are neat and uniform. You can use more than one color quilting thread on the same quilt.

Sometimes a student will ask to use a dark navy, a dark green or a burgundy thread on a white or muslin fabric so as to incorporate a color being used someplace else in the quilt. What happens with the very dark threads on a very light fabric is that the thread just looks black. There isn't enough surface color on one strand of thread to give the intended effect of bringing color to the fabric. If the effect of color is desired, use the pastel thread of the same color to bring just a touch of color across.

The colored threads are therefore used more to blend with the fabrics you are quilting so as not to accentuate each stitch, than to add color to the quilt top. Very busy fabrics will prohibit the threads from being seen in any event, so when using them, you will just want to choose a traditional color or one which will go nicely with all the fabrics you have in your quilt. If I have a choice of thread colors to use, I use the color which blends the best with the solid fabric in the quilt. If using two or more solid fabrics, I may even change quilting thread colors to correspond with each solid. If doing this, I would use a busy backing so that these changes would not be offensive on the back of the quilt.

QUILTING THIMBLES

For all of you out there who say, "I can't sew with a thimble," trust me, you will learn. I was one of those who put the thimble on the finger I was supposed to push the needle with and immediately pushed with the finger which had no thimble on it. I even learned how to push the needle through with the nail on my finger, so I wouldn't have to use a thimble. Eventually, the nail gave way with a very unattractive hole through it.

Some quilters even quilt with two thimbles – one to push the needle through and one underneath the quilt for the needle to bounce off. Many quilters use just their bare finger underneath to feel the pressure of the needle coming through and develop a callous on their finger from this noble task. I don't quilt with two thimbles, but I am not quite so noble. When my finger underneath is feeling a little worn out, I put a tab of cloth adhesive tape on this finger to give it a buffer between it and the needle coming through.

When selecting the one or two thimbles you will be using, you have many options.

LEATHER THIMBLES: These thimbles are often used by the "I can't use a thimble group." They are not too difficult for most people to become accustomed to. They tend to mold to the finger. When you quilt with a leather thimble, you push the needle with the side of your finger rather than the top. They also wear out from use and need to be replaced. I began quilting with a leather thimble, but after I wore through enough of them to decorate a Christmas tree, I decided I should take my own advice and learn how to use a metal thimble.

TRADITIONAL METAL THIMBLES: The traditional metal thimble with deep dimples in the top for pushing the needle is probably the most common thimble used by quilters. For me, attempting to go from my favorite leather thimble to a traditional thimble was not an easy task. For one thing, it took me a long time to realize that I needed to put more pressure on the metal thimble in order to manipulate the needle, than I had with the leather thimble. The other problem I had was long nails. If I could find a thimble which would accommodate my finger, it was not deep enough to accommodate my nails.

TAILOR'S THIMBLES: Bingo! Here was a hard metal thimble which would not wear out and had the top cut off so my nail could poke through. I was pushing with the side of the thimble, so I didn't need the top of the thimble anyway. Obviously, those who have the quilting style of pushing with the top of the thimble need a traditional thimble.

RAISED EDGE THIMBLES: These are used like the traditional thimble, but with a raised edge to trap the needle. They are also used under the quilt where the thin edge is used to bounce the needle point off.

HAND-HELD THIMBLES: This is a small metal tool recently introduced on the market which you would grasp in your hand and use to push the needle through. Again, if you have the opportunity to try one, see what you think.

As with any other task, the preferred method or tool is the one you feel most comfortable with, and find works best for you. I graduated to the tailor's thimble from necessity. When it was necessary for me to put the effort in to learn to use it, I did. Put in the effort with the type of thimble which you think might fill your needs best.

Figure 12-1

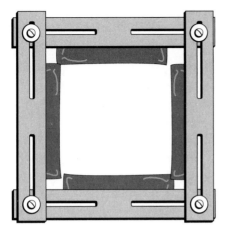

HOOPS AND FRAMES

Most quilters, not all, use a hoop or frame to stretch the three basted layers in order to quilt. I caution you that in the beginning you may want to forego the frame because it inhibits your ability to quilt, or so you think. Actually, if you don't use a frame, you really are weaving the fabric on the needle. The purpose of the frame is to hold the three layers stationary and taut as you manipulate the fabric with your fingers and push the needle through. Stick with the frame at first and once you feel comfortable quilting you can give a go at quilting without a frame. At that point, you will be familiar enough with quilting to know if quilting without a frame is for you.

HOOPS: Quilting hoops come in various sizes and are generally made of wood. Do not confuse them with the weaker wooden embroidery hoops. You need a hoop which is small enough to catch the perimeter of a square if you are working on a small project. If you are working on a full size quilt, I would suggest you start with a 14" to 18" hoop. Again, your personal preference will be important. The smaller the hoop, the easier it is to manipulate, but the more often you will have to move it in order to quilt a given area. The larger the hoop, the more unwieldy, but the fewer times it will be necessary to move. Reach a comfortable compromise.

QUILT-AS-YOU-GO FRAMES: These are frames which are used to quilt individual blocks that are used for pillows or are joined together after they are quilted to make a larger project.

They are usually made of four pieces of wood which have fabric attached that you can pin your square to. These frames generally adjust to a wide range of sizes and are fine for those small projects and quilt-as-you-go projects. (Figure 12-1)

LARGE FLOOR FRAMES: Oddly enough many people think that you have to quilt all quilts on large frames which sit in the middle of the house. Indeed, years ago many quilts were quilted on the large frames and often many hands would work on the same quilt at the same time. Today, many women continue to quilt at a large frame. Most quilters who do quilt at a large frame, though, learn to quilt in all directions. They can quilt away from themselves, toward themselves, to the right and to the left. This is necessary because otherwise they would be leaping from one side of the frame to the other, each time their quilting line changed direction. I used to quilt at the floor frame and consequently learned to quilt in all directions. Now, I opt for the lap hoop so that the quilt frame is not something my family needs to dodge. The lap hoop also allows me to quilt in the kitchen, the family room while watching TV, the bedroom when I want to relax and at a friend's home when I want to socialize. I have even quilted in the front seat of the car when I had a deadline. The hoop makes quilting very portable.

DECIDING WHERE TO BEGIN QUILTING

Begin right in the middle. You want to place the hoop in the middle of the quilt and begin quilting from the center out. You will want to move your hoop around the center area of the quilt so as not to constantly be pulling in one direction. (Figure 12-2)

Quilting is not a hot summer activity. It feels wonderful to have a basted quilt draped around you in the cool months, but not so wonderful in July. Don't start quilting your first quilt in June.

BEGINNING THE QUILTING

The center of the quilt is stretched in a hoop or frame. It does not need to be really taut. You will need to manipulate the fabric with your fingers and if the quilt is too tightly stretched, you will not be able to. If you find it is too tight in the hoop, just give it a punch in the center to loosen it up. (This is also a good way to get rid of your aggressions!)

Thread your quilting needle with approximately 15" of quilting thread.

Figure 12-2

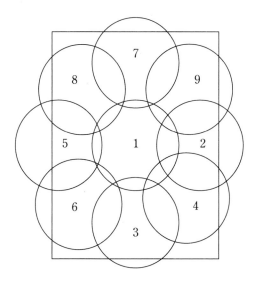

TRICK

Thread has a twist, so it matters which end is threaded on the needle. If you are right handed, thread your needle right from the spool, pulling out the desired length, cutting it and knotting the end you just cut. If you are left handed, pull the desired amount off the spool, cut it and thread the needle with the end just cut. If you are right handed and want to be lightning fast at your quilting, you can thread several quilting needles onto a spool of thread and pull one needle off at a time with thread.

Figure 12-3

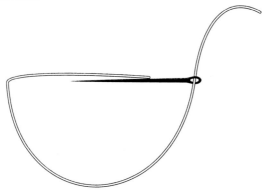

MAKING A NICE LITTLE KNOT

I know you probably think I am going overboard here, but this technique makes a nice, dry, little knot of consistent size each time and is well worth learning.

• Take the long tail of the single thread and lay it along side the needle. (Figure 12-3)

• Wrap the thread around the needle four times. (Figure 12-4)

• Pull the needle through while holding the wrapped area between two fingers till it reaches the end of the thread. (Figure 12-5)

• Whammo! You have made a nice, neat knot. (Figure 12-6)

Figure 12-4

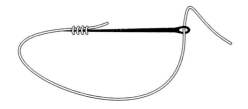

Figure 12-5

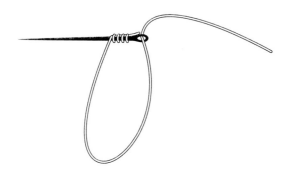

Figure 12-6

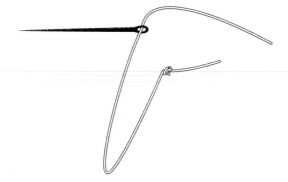

You are ready to begin quilting. Slide the needle in between the layers, (not through to the back) about 1" away from where you want to begin quilting. When you come up, give a little tug so that the knot will slip in between the layers. (Figure 12-7)

Figure 12-7

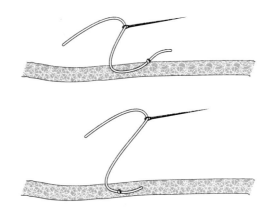

TRICK

If the knot does not want to come through easily, place your nail on it to hold it down and try again. The counter pressure against the knot holds the fabric and the knot taut and aids in pulling it into the fabric. (Figure 12-8)

Figure 12-8

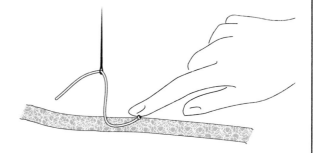

If the tail of the thread behind the knot is still on the top of the quilt, place the point of your needle in between the layers and sweep the needle to pull it down. (Figure 12-9)

Figure 12-9

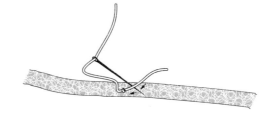

Figure 12-10

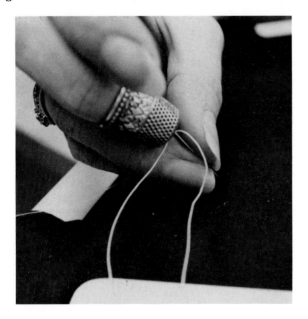

QUILTING TOWARDS YOU WITH THE ROCKER QUILTING STITCH

This is probably the most common method used in quilting.

• Put the needle straight into the fabric with two fingers (probably the thumb and another finger). It is important to put the needle straight down rather than at an angle so that your stitches on the back side of the quilt will be the approximate size of the stitches on the top of the quilt. (Figure 12-10)

• Push the needle through until you feel the needle point with the tip of the finger which has been placed underneath the quilt hoop. We are not looking to draw blood. You only want to feel the pressure of it coming through. As soon as you feel the needle point, drop the needle down to the quilt and push up on the fabric from underneath along the shank of the needle just behind the point. (Figure 12-11)

Figure 12-11

• At the same time, you are now guiding the needle with the thimble and the thumb is pushing down from the top so as to form a crease through which the needle will push. (Figure 12-12)

You have just taken one stitch, don't rest on your laurels and don't pull the needle through but do repeat the process one more time. I always tell new quilters to put two stitches of equal length on the needle and then pull the needle through. You want to take at least those two stitches so you can begin to establish that rhythm. Once you begin to feel comfortable, take three stitches on the needle. Then work up to four. If you have established this rhythm, your stitches should be even and consistent. When you are pulling the thread through the fabric, you want to pull it tight enough that the design is evident, but not so tight that the fabric gathers. Remember that the stitches will look larger on the needle than they will look in the fabric. (Figure 12-13)

Now, practice, practice and practice until you start to get the hang of it.

This is commonly called the rocker quilting stitch.

Learn to quilt in one direction and when you feel comfortable, learn to quilt in the other. Try towards you and if that doesn't seem to feel comfortable try quilting away from you.

Figure 12-12

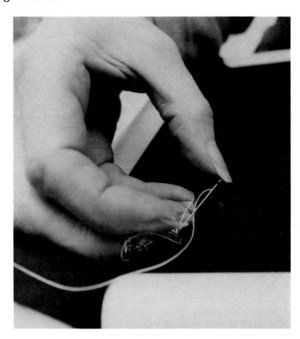

Figure 12-13

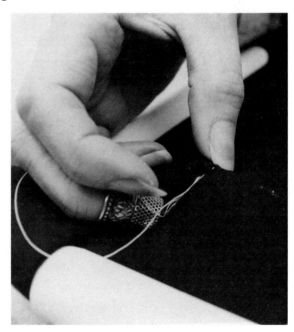

Figure 12-14

Figure 12-15

Figure 12-16

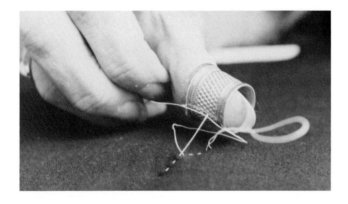

Figure 12-17

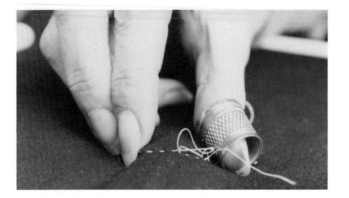

QUILTING AWAY FROM YOU

Quilting away from you is done exactly the same way except your thumb is responsible for pushing the needle through and your first finger is responsible for pushing the fabric down. (Figure 12-14, 12-15, 12-16, 12-17)

TRICK

A way to speed up your quilting is to save time pulling the length of your thread through only after you have filled your needle twice. Load the needle and pull it through only to the point where you can load it again. Since you have filled your needle twice, pull the thread through to the end. (Figure12-18)

Figure 12-18

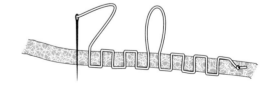

STAB STITCHING

There is another method of quilting called stab stitching. With this method, the quilter pushes the needle straight down from the top to the underside of the quilt, where it is grabbed by the other hand and fed back up through to the top. For most quilters, the stitch taken on top of the quilt is fine, but the stitch on the back is uneven except for those who are most skilled in this method. Since each stitch is taken one at a time, it is a much slower method.

There are times, however, when the stab stitch is used by those who normally use the rocker stitch. When an area has an excessive amount of seam allowances and the needle cannot rock through the bulk, the stab stitch is the alternate method.

SLIDING THROUGH TO OTHER AREAS

Rather than starting and stopping at each place there is quilting, you can slide your needle underneath between the layers to begin quilting in a new area.

If the distance is just a bit longer, you can carefully rotate the point of the needle further and come up at that point.

DECIDING WHEN TO END THE THREAD

When you have reached the end of a line of quilting and you can't slide the needle between the layers to another quilting area, it is time to end the thread.

If you have about six inches of thread on the needle, you will need to end the thread.

You do not need to end the thread just because you are at the edge of the hoop or frame. You simply pull your needle out and leave the thread dangling to re-thread a needle once the frame has been moved to its area. Or, you may leave the needle loaded with stitches in the quilt at the edge of the hoop to be picked up once the hoop has been moved.

When going further than you can reach the needle, slide the needle between the layers, come up with the point only halfway. Grasping the point, turn the eye of the needle still lodged between the layers in the direction you want to go and with a hard thimble, push the eye of the needle up through the fabric in the desired location. (Figure12-19, 12-20, 12-20)

Figure 12-19

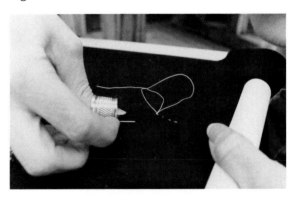

Figure 12-20

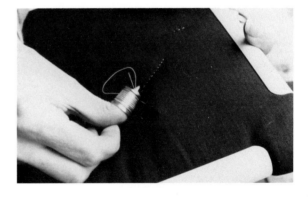

Figure 12-21

Figure 12-22

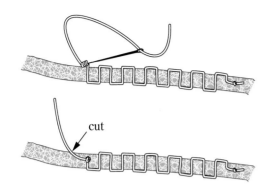

cut

Figure 12-23

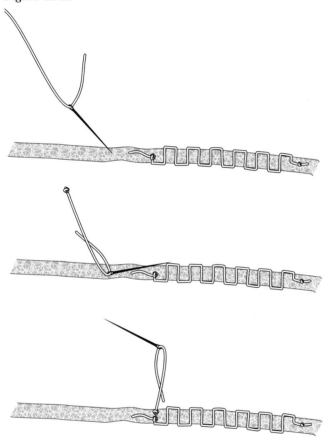

ENDING THE THREAD

To end a thread, place your needle close to the top of the quilt where the thread is coming up, wrap the thread around it three or four times and pull the needle through while holding on to the French knot-type wraps. Once the small knot is on the thread, put the needle back in the same hole the thread is coming from but only between the layers, pop the knot inside and cut the thread. If I am still going to continue to quilt, I pop it through along the quilting line, so I will then quilt over the loose end. (Figure 12-22)

To begin a new thread, insert the needle and knotted thread about 1" away from the ending hole. Come up in that ending hole with the thread and take a tiny backstitch through the top only before you continue quilting. By using this method, the stitch is complete on both the top and the bottom. (Figure 12-23)

Some quilters prefer to also take a backstitch in this area when ending and making their knots. (Figure 12-24)

Figure 12-24

QUILTING TRICKS

• Start quilting in an area where you will be able to continue quilting for as long a possible without ending. (Figure 12-25)

• Quilt interlocking designs when possible so you can continue to quilt. (Figure 12-26)

• When quilting long lines that run together, quilt with several needles and leave them in the top to be picked up when the hoop or frame is moved. (Figure 12-27)

Figure 12-25

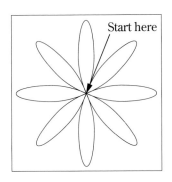

Figure 12-26

Not this

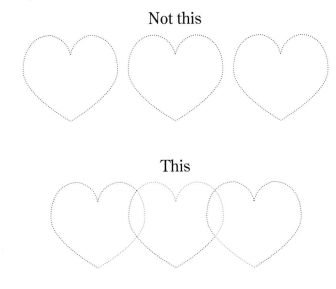

This

Figure 12-27

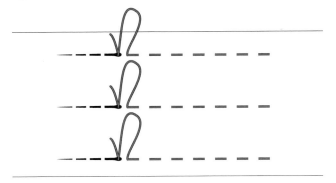

Figure 12-28

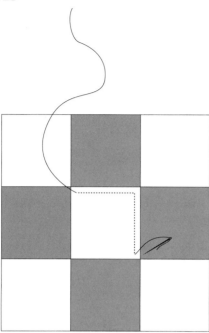

• When quilting in the center of a design area, cut your thread twice as long and quilt off in one direction. When finished re-thread the other end and quilt with it. (Figure 12-28)

• Leave your quilting out with a threaded needle that is ready for quilting. (Being a mother, I hasten to add: but out of reach of small children.) This inviting scene will make you want to quilt, even if only to sit down and relax for 15 minutes. The quilt will get quilted before you know it. A quilt can be like the blender in the cabinet that never gets used because it's too much trouble to get it ready. If it is out and ready to go, you will quilt. If it is under the bed or in the closet, it doesn't come to mind, and even if it does, you will opt to do something handy.

• Set goals for yourself where your quilting is concerned. A quilter with goals has finished quilts. When deciding what and where to quilt, estimate the time it will take you to complete your project, so you are well aware of the commitment you are undertaking.

I know one friend who was insistent that the quilt would be on the bed by a certain date. It was not quite done, so she put it on the bed and finished the quilting a little bit each night as she lay in bed, while her husband did his reading. Needles in bed, I don't recommend, but her goals were almost met.

Remember, quilting is supposed to be fun and relaxing. Don't let yourself become frustrated by this new skill you are learning. Just concentrate on the mechanics and once you have the mechanics down, just practice. I can guarantee that the more you quilt, the better you will become. Use the time you spend quilting your quilt to relax and enjoy the process. I think it must be the rhythm which develops that seems to really relax me when I quilt. When I began each day with 30 to 40 minutes of quilting, I would go over in my mind the things I needed to accomplish that day and organize my day in the most efficient way. If I was really tired in the evening, I would quilt and just let my mind wander and unwind. If I need to "think of something," like a name for the quilt, etc., the time spent quilting allows time to ponder ideas and affords me the luxury of a relaxing period of time.

Chapter Thirteen

Bindings
and Other Finishings

Figure 13-1

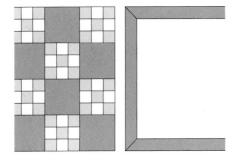

Once the entire quilt has been quilted, it will be necessary for you to finish the outer edges. There are several ways to do this.

BRINGING THE TOP
AROUND TO THE BACK

This method is not done on quilts which are designed to be used on a bed, but may be an option for a quilted article made for display where you do not want the finished edge shown on the front. To do this, you need to trim the backing and the batting to approximately ½" to ¾" shorter than the top all around the edge. Turn under ¼" of the top and then bring it around to the back and do a blind stitch through the batting but not through the front. (Figure 13-1)

Figure 13-2

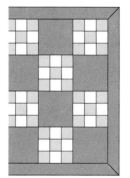

BRINGING THE BACK AROUND TO THE FRONT

This method is sometimes called a "self binding." It is done just the opposite from the first method. Trim the batting flush with the top of the quilt. Cut the backing evenly ½" to ¾" out from the top and batting, all around the perimeter. Turn ¼" under and then bring the back around to the front and blind stitch it in place. With this method I *do* allow the stitch to go all the way through to the back of the quilt. It gives the appearance of a more defined edge. You *can* stitch only through to the batting if you like. This method is frequently used for quick or small projects, but again it is not the strongest or preferred edging. (Figure 13-2)

SEPARATE BINDINGS WHICH ARE SEWN ON BY THE SEWING MACHINE

Before we begin this portion, I want you to know that there is a gadget that you can put on your Christmas list. You will have a perfect answer for those who say you are so hard to buy for. It is called a "Walking Foot" or an "Even Feed Foot" for your sewing machine. The purpose of this foot is to evenly feed several layers through the sewing machine at the same rate. The top fabric is fed through with "feed dogs" at the same rate the bottom fabric is being pulled through with its "feed dogs." Using this attachment on your sewing machine when you are sewing separate bindings allows the three layers to be pulled through at the same rate.

To put a separate binding on the quilt, all the layers of the quilt should be cut flush with the top's edges.

USING STRAIGHT GRAIN OR BIAS BINDING

If you are binding a straight edge, you can use straight grain or bias grain binding.

If you are binding a curved edge, you must use bias grain binding so the binding will have the "give" to go around the curves.

CUTTING STRAIGHT GRAIN BINDING

Straight grain binding is cut either across the width or down the length of a piece of fabric. Several strips are cut and seamed together in one long strip which is a little longer than the perimeter of your quilt. If you have the length of fabric, you may also cut four separate strips to correspond with the four sides and miter the four corners separately. The easiest way to cut these strips would be with a marked ruler and the rotary cutter discussed earlier. There are two ways to use this straight grain strip, single fold and double fold.

MAKING CONTINUOUS SINGLE-FOLD STRAIGHT GRAIN BINDING

Single fold binding would require that the strip be cut wide enough to turn ¼" under on the front, have the desired width showing on the front (usually around ¼"), have the desired width showing on the back (again, usually around ¼") and turn under the ¼" on the back. If you used the ¼" showing on the front and back, your strip would need to be cut 1" wide and a seamed length long enough to go around the perimeter of the quilt. (Figure 13-3)

Once the strip has been cut, press under ¼" all along one long side. To sew on a continuous single-fold straight-grain binding, begin along the side of the quilt. (Any side will do, but I usually like to begin in the least obvious place such as along a random spot on the bottom portion of the quilt. Don't aim for dead center of any side where your eye might be drawn.) Placing the edge which has *not* been pressed along the edge of the quilt, with right sides and raw edges together, begin sewing about 3" from the beginning of the strip and ¼" in from the edge. (Figure 13-4)

The very first thing you will come to is a corner. Since corners have tricks and methods all their own, I am not going to discuss those here but further on in the chapter. Continue to sew until you are 2" to 3" from the beginning of the binding strip. Bring both loose ends together with right sides together just so they meet and pin. With a pencil and ruler, mark the desired seam line and sew. Trim away the excess and place the joined binding back down along the edge of the quilt and continue to sew to your beginning stitching. (Figure 13-5)

Figure 13-3

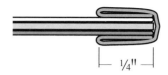

Figure 13-4

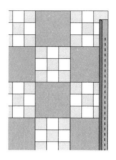

Figure 13-5

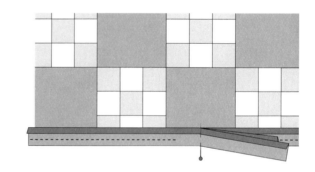

Figure 13-6

Figure 13-7

MAKING CONTINUOUS DOUBLE FOLD STRAIGHT GRAIN BINDING

The width of the strip cut for this type of a binding would be ½" on the front for seam allowance (you will only be seeing ¼" in from the edge but the strip has been folded so it is actually double, or ½"), ½" showing (again, you only will have ¼" showing on the front but the fabric is folded so it is double), and then another ½" showing on the back (again only ¼" will actually show, but you need ½" since it is folded). You will not need a seam allowance in the back because you have a folded edge. O.K., this means that to sew ¼" in, having ¼" showing on the front and another ¼" showing on the back, you need to cut a strip for double-fold in the 1½" to 2" wide range. Sometimes, if I have a pieced edge on my quilt, the wider 2" strip is a little easier to handle. (Figure 13-6)

The strip is pressed in half lengthwise with wrong sides together. The folded strip is sewn along the edge of the quilt exactly as the single-fold was sewn. Again, we will deal with the question of corners a little further on.

MAKING CONTINUOUS BIAS BINDING

Continuous bias binding is done exactly as you would do continuous double-fold, straight-grain binding with the only difference being that the strips are cut along the bias grain of the fabric. (Figure 13-7)

I have used ¼" showing for example purposes, but you may use whatever width you prefer and feel is acceptable for your purposes. If you are wondering what is traditional, ¼" to ½" is traditional.

METHOD FOR MAKING
CONTINUOUS BIAS BINDING: This is a nice method whereby you can make whatever width strip of continuous binding you would like.

• Begin with a square of fabric. A 36" square of fabric will yield approximately 585 running inches of 2" wide bias. (Figure 13-8)

• Draw one diagonal line and mark each side 1 through 4 and cut on the line. (Figure 13-9)

Figure 13-8

Figure 13-9

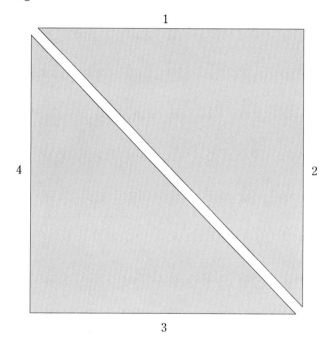

Figure 13-10

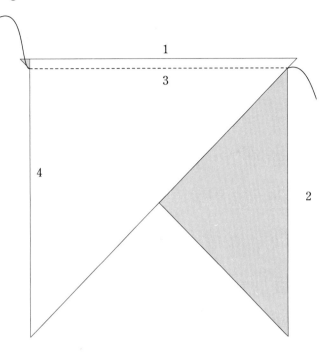

• Join sides 1 & 3 with right sides together, overlapping ends in order to sew with a ¼" seam allowance. (Figure 13-10)

• Place a lined or grided ruler along the bias edge in whatever width you would like the bias strips to be. Mark parallel lines the desired width on the wrong side of the fabric. (You will know which edges are bias by giving them a tug. The bias edges have lots of give and the straight edges have practically no give.) (Figure 13-11)

Figure 13-11

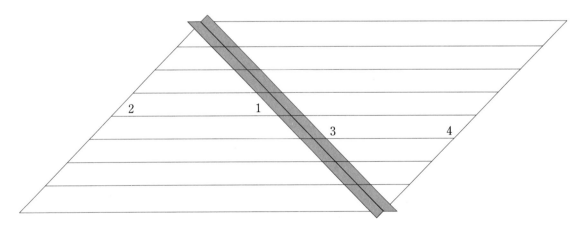

- Bring sides 2 and 4 together to form a tube. (Figure 13-12)
- Move one side of the tube down one line and begin to pin right sides together matching up the rest of the lines. The lines will actually cross each other. Pin at the point where they cross and sew with a ¼" seam allowance. (Figure 13-13)
- Open the seam and press. Cut along the lines. If it is a large fabric tube, I slip it over the end of the ironing board and rotate it as I cut it apart. (Figure 13-14)

I used to guess generously what size square was needed and save any leftover bias bindings for future projects. Now, I have taken the time to determine what size square to use to make the amount I need. Chapter 16 contains a chart for 1½" and 2" wide bias square requirements for varying lengths.

Figure 13-12

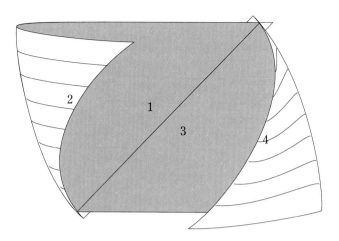

Figure 13-13

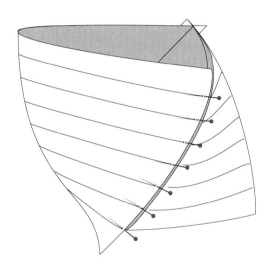

Figure 13-14

TRICK

If you want to get a quick rough estimate of how much bias a specific square size will yield, divide the square size by the width of your bias and multiply the whole number only of your answer times the square size again. For example: A 29" square divided by a 2" bias width equals 14.5. Now 14 times 29 equals 406. This means that a 29" square would yield approximately 406" of 2" wide bias.

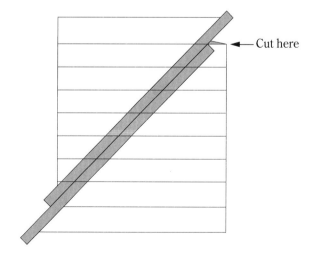

Cut here

Figure 13-15

Figure 13-16

Figure 13-17

CORNERS, CORNERS, CORNERS

I think when it comes to bindings and edges, the corners are always the areas most feared. One option you can use is to eliminate all your corners. This can be done by cutting all the corners into gentle curves. An easy way to curve corners is to place a large dinner plate across the corner and trace the curve. Keep in mind, if you curve your corners, you must use bias binding.

MITERING CORNERS AFTER SEWING ON THE BINDING: This method can be used with single- and double-fold straight grain binding and double-fold bias binding.

• As you are sewing your binding on, stop and backstitch about 2″ from the corner. Using your binding strip, measure the distance to the corner, add 2″ and then measure down the other side about 2″ and continue sewing on the binding. Work all four corners in this fashion. (Figure 13-15)

• Go back to the corner and bring right sides together, pin through both bindings and into corner where seam allowance would fall. (Figure 13-16)

• Draw a pencil line from first seam allowance to midpoint on the strip, flush with the edge of the quilt to the other seam allowance. (Figure 13-17)

• With the right sides together on the strip, sew the "arrow" on the strip. You will want to sew this arrow by hand at first until you feel comfortable with it. (Figure 13-18)

• Trim away excess fabric. (Figure 13-19)

• Lay strip back along edge and sew along each edge up to arrow. Be sure to backstitch. This can be sewn by hand or by machine. (Figure 13-20)

This method is well worth learning and makes a very nice corner on both the front and the back of the quilt.

Figure 13-18

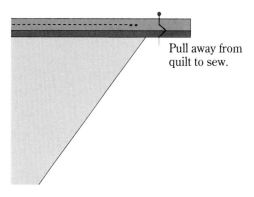

Pull away from quilt to sew.

Figure 13-19

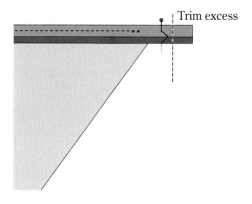

Trim excess

Figure 13-20

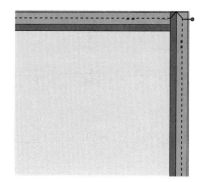

Figure 13-21

MITERING CORNERS WHILE SEWING ON THE BINDING: You can miter the corners of your quilt with your sewing machine as you are sewing the binding on. This method can be used with continuous single fold or continuous double-fold straight-grain and continuous fold bias.

• As you approach the first corner, stop and backstitch about 3" from the edge. (Figure 13-21)

• Fold the binding strip back on itself at the point where it reaches the corner. (Figure 13-22)

• Mark a 45° angle from the sewing line edge to the middle of the strip and out to the other edge. (Figure 13-23)

Figure 13-22

Figure 13-23

• Set your sewing machine stitch to about 12 to 14 stitches to the inch and sew along the marked line having the binding strip folded back upon itself. Backstitch at the beginning and end. (Figure 13-24, 13-25)

Figure 13-24

Figure 13-25

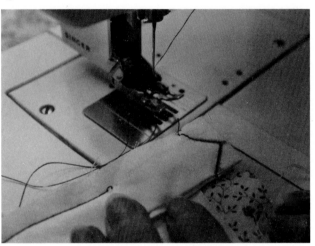

Figure 13-26

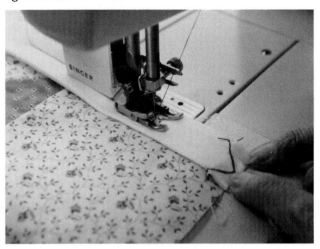

- Lay the opened binding strip back down along the edge and begin stitching where you left off. Continue to the middle of the corner which is the beginning of the miter stitching. (Figures 13-26, 13-27)

- Raise the needle and flip the seam allowance to the other side of the needle and drop the needle into the backside of the miter and continue to sew to the next corner. (Figures 13-28 & 13-29)

Figure 13-27

Figure 13-28

Figure 13-29

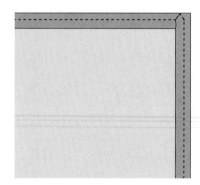

MITERING CORNERS WHEN USING SEPARATE STRIPS:

- To sew these mitered corners after all four strips are sewn, lay out both ends one on top of the other with wrong sides facing up. With your ruler mark a 45° line from the point where the stitching will or has intersected. (Figure 13-30)

- Now move your ruler and mark another line from the midpoint to the outside edge of the binding. (Figure 13-31)

- With right sides together, stitch by hand or by machine on the lines which form an arrow and trim excess fabric. (Figure 13-32)

- The binding may now be turned to the back and hand stitched.

Figure 13-30

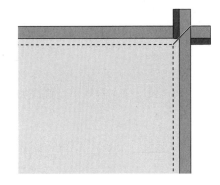

Figure 13-31

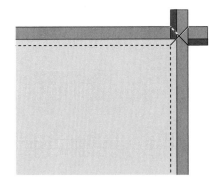

Figure 13-32

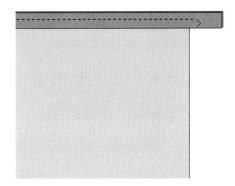

Figure 13-33

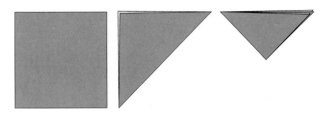

Figure 13-34

Figure 13-35

Fold edges

Figure 13-36

STITCHING THE BINDING TO THE BACK OF THE QUILT

All of the attached bindings need to be hand stitched on the back of the quilt. The blind stitch or slip stitch (those stitches used in applique) are used. It is important that the machine stitching used to sew the binding on is covered by the binding on the back. You do not want your hand stitches to be seen on the front of the quilt, so check frequently to see that your needle is not going all the way through to the front.

ADDING PRAIRIE POINTS

This is another method you can use to finish the edge with a more decorative approach. Prairie Points are separate pieces of fabric which are folded in a couple of different ways and sewn on to the top in a continuous fashion prior to the sandwiching process. There are two ways to make Prairie Points.

METHOD ONE:

- Fold and press squares of fabric as shown in the example. (Figure 13-33)
- Once you have a stack of folded triangles, join one to the other by opening the points of the last openings and slipping the fold of the next triangle inside and stitching along the base ⅛". Continue to join the triangles until you have a strip of points long enough to go around the perimeter of your project. (Figure 13-34)

METHOD TWO:

- Fold and press squares of fabric as follows: (Figure 13-35)
- Once you have a stack of folded triangles, join one to the other by placing one triangle atop the next where they meet at the base and stitch ⅛" along the base. Continue to sew until you have a strip long enough to go around the perimeter of your project. (Figure 13-36)

JOINING PRAIRIE POINTS TO THE QUILT TOP:

- Laying raw edges together, attach the prairie points along the edge of the quilt top by sewing ¼" in from the edge. As you approach the corners, measure your prairie point strip to see where you need to cut the stitching and either lengthen or shorten the spacing so the corners will meet in the following fashion. (Figure 13-37)

- As you approach the joining place of your beginning, clip the stitching to allow for the uniform placement of the points. (Figure 13-38)

- The quilt is then sandwiched, basted and quilted. To finish, the edge, bring the backing fabric up to just beyond the machine stitching, turning the backing edge under ¼" (trim if necessary), blind or slip stitch the backing to the prairie points. (Figure 13-39)

SIGNING YOUR WORK

Take the time to make a label for the back of your quilt which gives your name, the name of the quilt and the date that you made it. You may want to add other information such as who the quilt is made for or special sentiments. Your quilt is special and an expression of your creativity and expertise. Don't leave future generations guessing. This will give your quilt documentation for future generations. Also, by signing and dating your quilt, you have increased its value. This can be accomplished by writing or typing on a piece of fabric with a permanent pen or done more elaborately in stitchery.

Figure 13-37

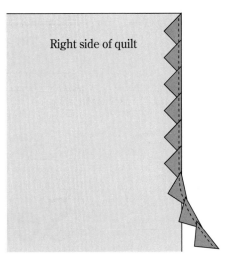

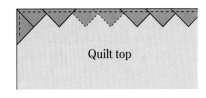

Figure 13-38

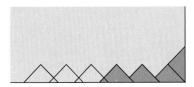

Figure 13-39

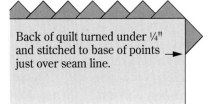

Back of quilt turned under ¼" and stitched to base of points just over seam line.

Chapter Fourteen

Sentiments and Thoughts

After spending countless hours putting down on paper all that I know about quilting and the answers to questions that I am most often asked about quilting, it seems rather anti-climactic to end this labor of love on "Bindings." The sentiments of quilting are as much a part of quilting as the mechanics. After all, it is not the mechanics of quilting which have drawn so many. It is the gratification of a job well done, the expression of one's artistic talents, the persistence of the quilter, or just the giving of oneself through the art of quilting, which has made quilting what it is. It is the ability to perhaps leave a little bit of yourself with others through your quilts.

Quilting is a vehicle which has drawn people together unlike any other craft. The quilting bees of yesterday where neighbors would get together and enjoy each other while their hands worked to create, are still going on today and are a big part of what quilting has to offer. Not until I sat at a floor frame for the first time with five other quilters did I experience this feeling.

Quilt guilds, organizations, shows and groups are stronger today than probably at any time in history. It is the sharing and love of quilting which has brought such satisfaction to so many. Often it is quilting that is the vehicle which affords quilters the opportunity to work together for worthwhile projects.

I treasure the quilts I have made, but I treasure most the very good friends I have had the good fortune to enjoy quilting with. The wonderful trips we have made to take classes, to enjoy quilt shows and still find time to enjoy each other, are some of my most treasured moments. If I had not become involved in quilting, I doubt that my life would feel as rich as it does. Few art and craft forms seem to enjoy this sharing and support given readily by quilters. You only need to step into your local quilt shop to hear the "quilt talk" going on to know that quilters are always ready to help one another.

Quilts made and raffled off to support good causes and quilts made and given as gifts of love and tribute attest to the sharing that quilters feel is a big part of their craft.

The local quilt shows and the enormous national and international shows are testament to the fact that quilters enjoy sharing their work with others. They are a wonderful source of inspiration to new quilters and experienced quilters alike.

I hope that this book will help you in your pursuit of this rich art and I encourage you to seek out the guilds, the shops, the shows and treasured quilt friends.

My hope is that this book will give you a sense of organization to your quilting, some new avenues to explore and the confidence to please yourself first.

May all your quilts be comforts.

Appendices

Appendix I

Making A Quick Sampler Quilt

Making a patchwork quilt seems like a huge project to many. I like to say that a quilt is only so many pillows. For this reason, I developed a very simple sampler quilt to be used in the beginning quilting classes that I teach. The sampler quilts have a minimum of squares and use borders and framing to make them large enough to be practical for beds. Your first quilt should be simple enough to be completed in a relatively short period of time, so you won't become bogged down.

The premise behind both the twin size and queen size sampler quilts is to make a few blocks in order to practice drafting, piecing and applique techniques. Then these blocks can be joined with strips of fabrics quickly in order to form your quilt so you can practice your quilting.

The yardage requirements given for both these quilts yield enough fabric to cut the fabric that you are going to use in the borders and framing *first*. Then the remaining fabric is used as you create the blocks for the quilt.

BINDINGS

You will have enough fabric to bind your quilts with either Fabric A or Fabric B. You may want to cut your binding strips for straight grain or the square for bias binding prior to cutting out the pieces for the patchwork blocks.

THE SCALED QUILT DRAWING

The scaled drawing of the twin size quilt and the queen size quilt will be your plan. Since each square equals 1", you can easily modify this drawing and visually determine your requirements by counting the squares. If your modifications require that you make templates, the full size templates can be made by using the actual 1" dimension per scaled square.

Twin Size Quick Sampler Quilt
Overall Size 64" x 88"

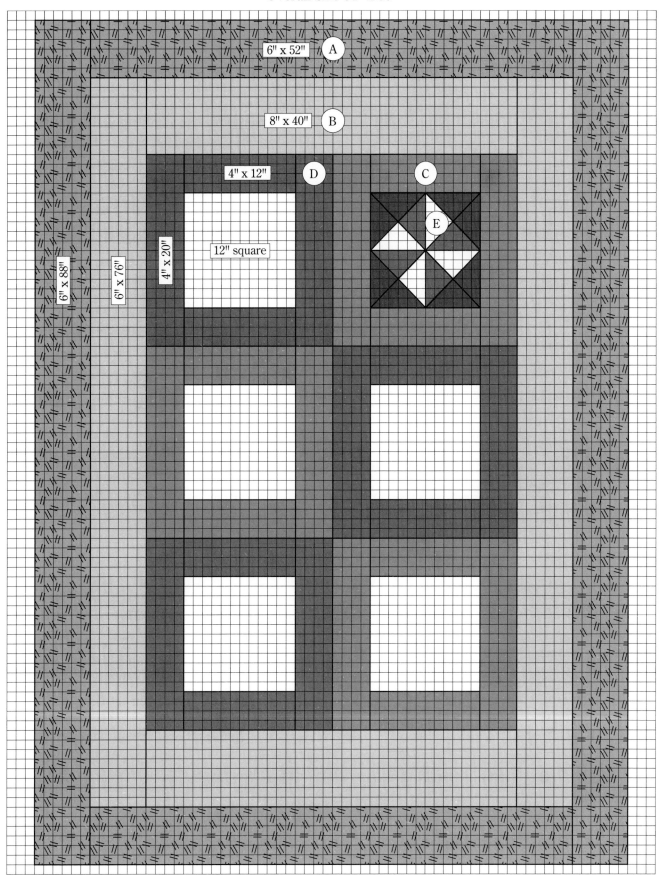

6" x 52" — A

8" x 40" — B

4" x 12" — D   C

12" square

4" x 20"

6" x 88"

6" x 76"

E

☐ = One inch

Figure 15-1

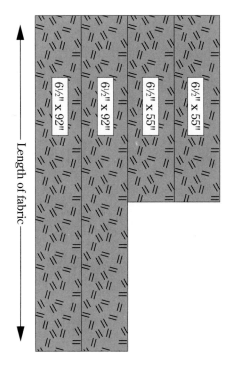

Figure 15-2

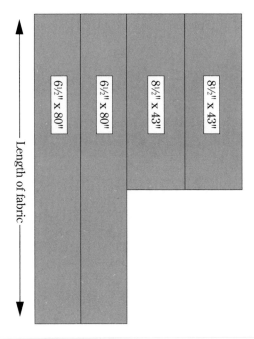

THE TWIN SIZE QUICK SAMPLER QUILT

FABRIC REQUIREMENTS:

Fabric A – 3 yards.

This fabric is used for the last border on the quilt. I like to make this fabric one of my darkest fabrics as it will act as a frame around the entire quilt. This could be a stripe or a large print. It could also be a calico with many of the colors used in the quilt. It could be a little print where pretty quilting would show.

Cut (down the length of the fabric):
- Two strips 6½" x 92" (the sides)
- Two strips 6½" x 55" (the top and bottom)

These strips will be several inches longer than is required on the drawing, to give you a little insurance policy. Since you are pre-cutting the strips before the quilt is actually completed, cut them a little longer just in case the quilt gets larger as it is being made. Hopefully, the quilt will measure the exact size it is suppose to, but just in case, you have the extra length. (Figure 15-1)

Fabric B – 2½ yards

This fabric is used at the inside border. It needs to contrast with Fabrics C and D as well as Fabric A, as these are the fabrics it will be next to. (Figure 15-2)

Cut (down the length of the fabric):
- Two strips 6½" x 80" (sides)
- Two strips 8½" x 43" (top and bottom)

Fabric C – 1½ yards

This fabric is used to frame three of the 12" patchwork blocks. Since this fabric will act as a frame, you might want to use a mini-print or a calico that isn't too busy. This fabric will be next to Fabric B and Fabric D so it will need to contrast with these two fabrics.

Cut:
- Six strips 4½" x 12½" (top and bottom)
- Six strips 4½" x 20½" (sides)

Since these strips are going to be added to your patchwork block, you will cut them the exact unfinished size and mark your seam lines the exact ¼" measurement. Should your patchwork blocks end up being a little larger or smaller than the exact 12" finished size, you will ease or stretch your blocks to fit these strips. (Figure 15-3)

Fabric D – 1½ yards

This fabric is used just like Fabric C, so you would cut the same number and size pieces as you did for Fabric C.

Fabric E – 1½ yards

This is your lightest fabric and is not used in any of the borders or framing, so you will not need to pre-cut any pieces. Since the fabrics A through D are all dark or medium color fabrics, you will want a lighter fabric or several lighter or darker fabrics to use in contrast with Fabrics A through D for your patchwork squares. Fabric E can actually be several pieces of different fabric which total and 1½ yards which you will use in your patchwork squares.

BACKING FABRIC: You may want to purchase fabric for the back of the quilt while you are buying the others. You will need six yards for the backing. That is two strips 3 yards long seamed down the middle. You will have plenty of excess backing fabric which can also be used in the top of the quilt.

STEPS TO MAKING THE TWIN SIZE
SAMPLER QUILT:
- Purchase fabric.
- Wash and iron fabric.
- Pre-cut strips for Fabrics A through D.
- Choose six patchwork blocks and complete in 12" finished size.
- Frame your patchwork blocks with Fabrics C and D.
- Join the framed blocks as per diagram.
- Add top and bottom borders with Fabric B.
- Add side borders with Fabric B.
- Add top and bottom borders with Fabric A.
- Add side borders with Fabric A.
- Press top and clip any loose threads.
- Mark quilting design on top.
- Seam backing fabric.
- Sandwich quilt with batting and backing and baste.
- Starting in the middle, quilt.
- Attach binding and finish.
- Add your label to the back of the quilt giving the name of the quilt, your name and the date completed.
- *Enjoy the fruits of your labor.*

Figure 15-3

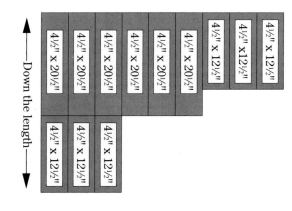

QUEEN SIZE QUICK SAMPLER QUILT
Overall size 84" x 92"

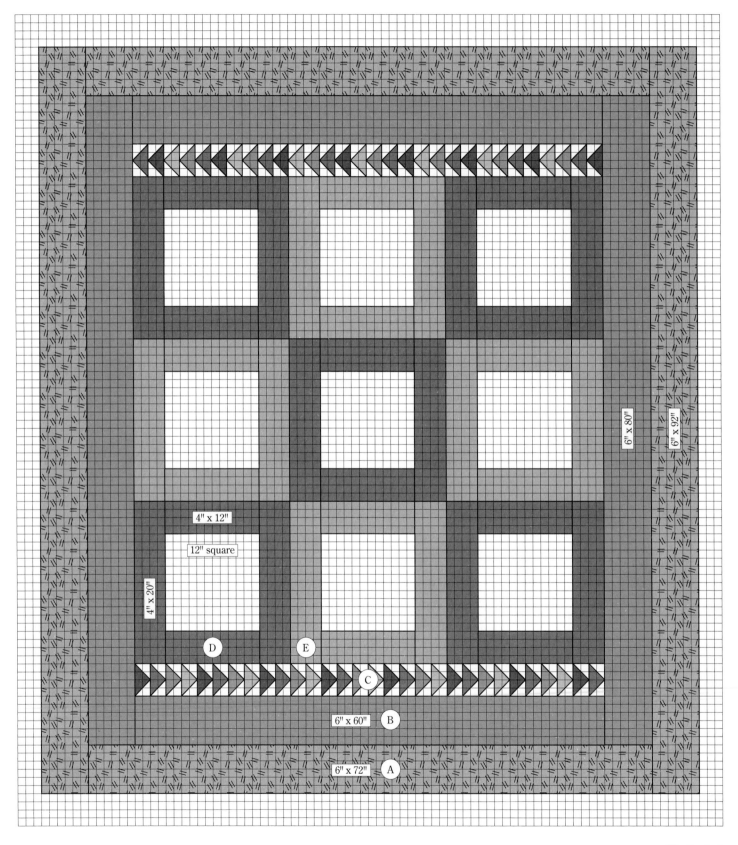

□ = One inch

THE QUEEN SIZE QUICK SAMPLER QUILT

The scaled drawing for the queen size shows that nine patchwork blocks are used and a pieced border of flying geese is added to the top and bottom of the quilt. Again, since you have this visual plan, you can make any modification you would like.

FABRIC REQUIREMENTS:

Fabric A – 3 yards

This fabric is used for the last border on the quilt. I like to make this fabric one of my darkest fabrics as it will act as a frame around the entire quilt. This could be a stripe or a large print. It could also be a calico with many of the colors used in the quilt. It could be a little print where pretty quilting would show.

Cut (down the length of the fabric):
- Two strips 6½" x 95" (the sides)
- Two strips 6½" x 75" (the top and bottom)

You will notice that I have instructed you to cut the strips several inches longer than is required on the drawing. The reason for this is to give you a little insurance policy. Since we are pre-cutting the strips before the quilt is actually completed, cut them a little longer just in case the quilt gets larger as it is being made. Hopefully, the quilt will measure the exact size it is supposed to, but just in case you have the extra length. (Figure 15-4)

Fabric B – 2½ yards

This fabric is used as the inside border. It needs to contrast with Fabrics C, D and E as well as Fabric A, as these are the fabrics it will be next to. (Figure 15-5)

Cut (down the length of the fabric)
- Two strips 6½" x 83" (sides)
- Two strips 6½" x 63" (top and bottom)

Fabric D – 2 yards

This fabric is used to frame five of the 12" patchwork blocks. Since this fabric will act as a frame, you might want to use a mini-print or a calico that isn't too busy. This fabric will be next to Fabric C, E and Fabric B so it will need to contrast with these three fabrics.

Cut:
- 10 strips 4½" x 12½" (top and bottom)
- 10 strips 4½" x 20½" (sides)

Figure 15-4

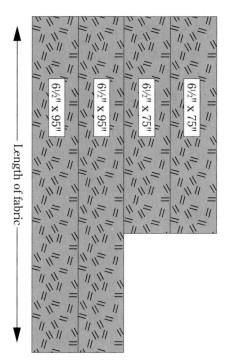

Figure 15-5

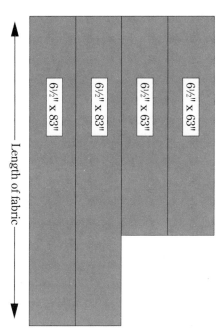

Figure 15-6

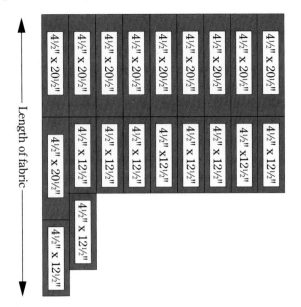

Length of fabric

4½" x 20½" (repeated for top row)
4½" x 12½" (middle row)
4½" x 20½"
4½" x 12½"
4½" x 12½"

Since these strips are going to be added to your patchwork block, you will cut them the *exact* unfinished size and mark your seam lines the *exact* ¼" measurement. Should your patchwork blocks end up being a little larger or smaller than the exact 12" finished size, you will ease or stretch your blocks to fit these strips. (Figure 15-6)

Fabric E – 2 yards

This fabric is used just like Fabric D, except that you will be framing 4 blocks instead of five blocks.

Cut:

- 8 strips 4½" x 12½" (top and bottom)
- 8 strips 4½" x 20½" (sides)

Fabric C – 2 yards

Fabric C can actually be several pieces of fabric which total 2 yards which you will use in your patchwork. This is your lightest fabric(s) and is also used as the background color of flying geese borders on the top and bottom of the inside of the quilt. You will need to cut 120 triangles. These lighter triangles can be one fabric or several lighter fabrics. Since the other fabrics are all dark or medium color fabrics, you will want a lighter fabric or several lighter fabrics to use in contrast with your other fabrics for your patchwork. (Figure 15-7)

BACKING FABRIC: You may want to purchase fabric for the back of the quilt while you are buying the others. You will need six yards for the backing. That is two strips 3 yards long seamed down the middle.

Figure 15-7

4" x 2" Flying Geese Border

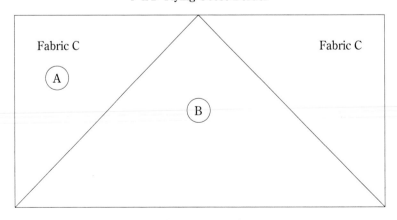

Fabric C   Fabric C
A
B

Template A – Actual size
Template B – Multi-colors

STEPS TO MAKING THE QUEEN SIZE QUICK SAMPLER QUILT:

- Purchase fabric.
- Wash and iron fabric.
- Pre-cut strips and triangles for Fabrics A–E.
- Choose nine patchwork blocks and complete in 12" finished size.
- Frame your patchwork blocks with Fabrics D and E.
- Join the framed blocks as per diagram.
- Piece two strips of 30 flying geese and add to top and bottom as per diagram.
- Add top and bottom borders with Fabric B.
- Add side border with Fabric B.
- Add top and bottom borders with Fabric A.
- Add side borders with Fabric A.
- Press top and clip any loose threads.
- Mark quilting design on top.
- Seam backing fabric.
- Sandwich quilt with batting and backing and baste.
- Starting in the middle, quilt.
- Attach binding and finish.
- Add your label to the back of the quilt giving the name of the quilt, your name and the date completed.
- *Enjoy the fruits of your labor.*

Helpful Charts and Information

STANDARD BED SIZES AND QUILT SIZES

When you are making a quilt for a particular purpose, the ideal situation is to measure the surface and the overhang and make your quilt to fit your measurements. You may however, want to make a coverlet or spread that fits standard sizes. Most of the quilts that I have made for beds have been comforters (fitting the top of the bed, with a 12" drop on the sides and bottom) rather than coverlets (fitting the top of the bed with 10" for pillow tuck and a 16" drop on the sides and bottom) or bedspreads (fitting the top of the bed with 10" for a pillow tuck and a 20" drop on the sides and bottom). The comforter size seems adequate and pillow shams can be made to match the quilt for a very pretty effect.

TYPE	MATTRESS SIZE	COMFORTER
Bassinet	13 x 28	13 x 28 or a little larger
Crib	23 x 46	36 x 50 blanket
Twin	39 x 75	63 x 87
Double	54 x 75	78 x 87
Queen	60 x 80	84 x 92
King	76 x 80	100 x 106

1½" BIAS STRIPS

LENGTH	SQUARE SIZE NEEDED
70"	11"
107"	13½"
140"	15"
189"	18"
240"	20"
300"	22"
360"	24"
432"	27"
500"	28"

2" BIAS STRIPS

LENGTH	SQUARE SIZE NEEDED
63"	12"
100"	15"
144"	18"
195"	20"
250"	23"
325"	27"
400"	29"
485"	32"
570"	34"
585"	36"

BIAS STRIP SQUARE SIZES

When you are making bias strips for a binding of a quilt via the quick method, it is helpful to know what size square you need to start with for your desired width and perimeter. Since 1½" and 2" appear to be the most popular widths made for the bias binding strips, I will list these in varying lengths.

Since the bias does stretch there is quite a bit of flexibility in the length. The formula given in Chapter Thirteen for estimating how much bias a specific size square will yield is also a helpful tool.

STRIP YARDAGES

Since many patchwork units and straight grain bindings are made from strips of fabric, it is helpful to know how many strips of fabric you can cut from a ½ yard or 1 yard piece for a particular width and how many running inches that will yield.

½ Yard (42" wide)

Strip Size	No. of Strips	Running Inches
1"	18 (exactly)	756
1½"	12 (exactly)	504
2"	9 (exactly)	378
2½"	7	294
3"	6 (exactly)	252
3½"	5	210
4"	4	168
4½"	4 (exactly)	168
5"	3	126
5½"	3	126
6"	3 (exactly)	126
6½"	2	84
7"	2	84
7½"	2	84
8"	2	84
9"	2 (exactly)	84

1 Yard (42" wide)

Strip Size	No. of Strips	Running Inches
1"	36 (exactly)	1,512
1½"	24 (exactly)	1,008
2"	18 (exactly)	756
2½"	14	588
3"	12	504
3½"	10	420
4"	9 (exactly)	378
4½"	8 (exactly)	336
5"	7	294
5½"	6	252
6"	6 (exactly)	252
6½"	5	210
7"	5	210
7½"	4	168
8"	4	168

Square Size	Triangle Size	Diagonal Measurement
1"	1"	1.41 or 1$\frac{7}{16}$"
1½"	1½"	2.12 or 2$\frac{1}{8}$"
2"	2"	2.83 or 2$\frac{13}{16}$"
2½"	2½"	3.54 or 3½"
3"	3"	4.24 or 4¼"
3½"	3½"	4.95 or 4$\frac{15}{16}$"
4"	4"	5.66 or 5⅝"
4½"	4½"	6.36 or 6⅜"
5"	5"	7.07 or 7$\frac{1}{16}$"
5½"	5½"	7.78 or 7¾"
6"	6"	8.49 or 8½"
6½"	6½"	9.19 or 9$\frac{3}{16}$"
7"	7"	9.90 or 9$\frac{15}{16}$"
7½"	7½"	10.61 or 10⅝"
8"	8"	11.31 or 11$\frac{5}{16}$"
8½"	8½"	12.02 or 12"
9"	9"	12.73 or 12¾"
9½"	9½"	13.44 or 13$\frac{7}{16}$"
10"	10"	14.14 or 14⅛"
10½"	10½"	14.85 or 14⅞"
11"	11"	15.56 or 15$\frac{9}{16}$"
11½"	11½"	16.26 or 16¼"
12"	12"	16.97 or 17"
12½"	12½"	17.68 or 17$\frac{11}{16}$"
13"	13"	18.39 or 18⅜"
13½"	13½"	19.09 or 19$\frac{1}{16}$"
14"	14"	19.80 or 19$\frac{13}{16}$"
14½"	14½"	20.51 or 20½"
15"	15"	21.21 or 21¼"
15½"	15½"	21.92 or 21$\frac{15}{16}$"
16"	16"	22.63 or 22⅝"
16½"	16½"	23.33 or 23$\frac{5}{16}$"
17"	17"	24.04 or 24"
17½"	17½"	24.75 or 24¾"
18"	18"	25.46 or 25$\frac{7}{16}$"

FIGURING DIAGONAL MEASUREMENTS

As discussed in Chapter Four, the diagonal measurement across a square or right angle isosceles triangle (a right angle with two sides being equal) is helpful to know for drafting purposes. (Figure 16-1)

Because we are converting hundredths to sixteenths in order to use our ruler, it is necessary to round up or down to the nearest sixteenth. Fabric is somewhat flexible and can be eased or stretched to accommodate this.

You can use the above chart in the reverse if the measurement you have is the diagonal. Locate the nearest diagonal measurement in the third column to locate its corresponding triangle or square.

Example: If your diagonal measurement is 17" then you know that a 12" square or triangle would correspond. (Figure 16-2)

Figure 16-1

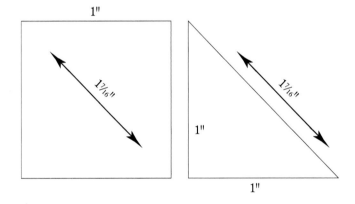

Figure 16-2

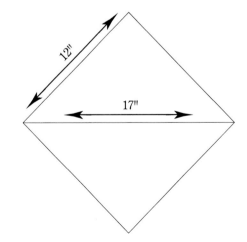

Appendix III

Full-Size
Applique Patterns

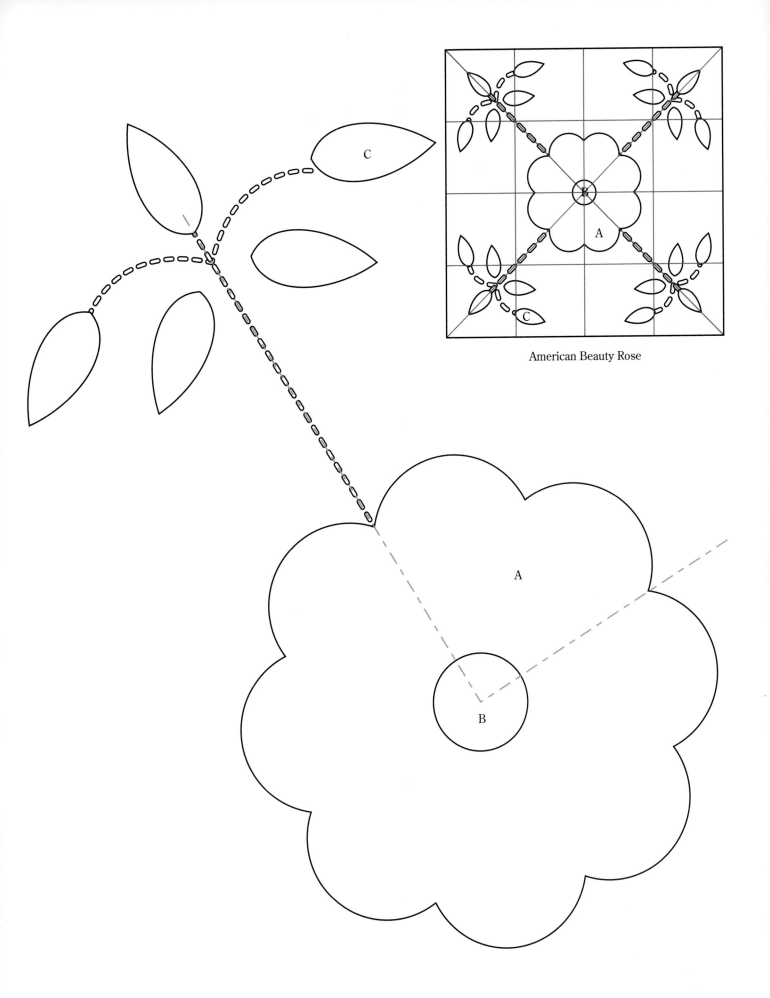

American Beauty Rose

Bride's Quilt

A

B

A

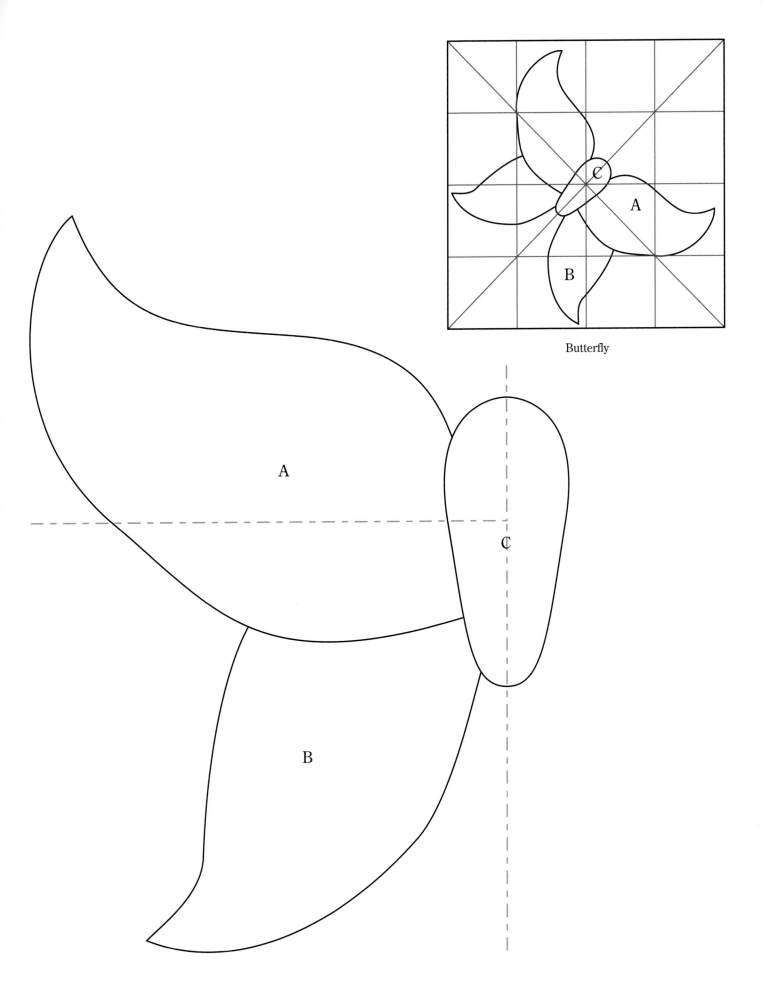

Butterfly

A

C

B

Lancaster Rose

Oak Leaf & Cherries

A

B

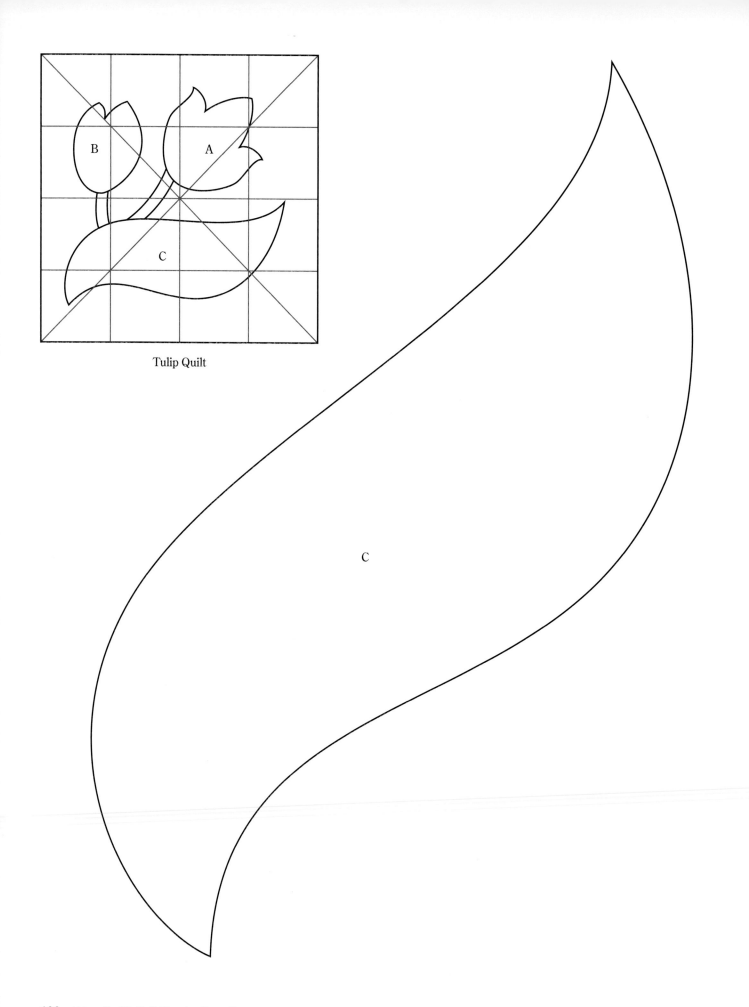

Tulip Quilt

C

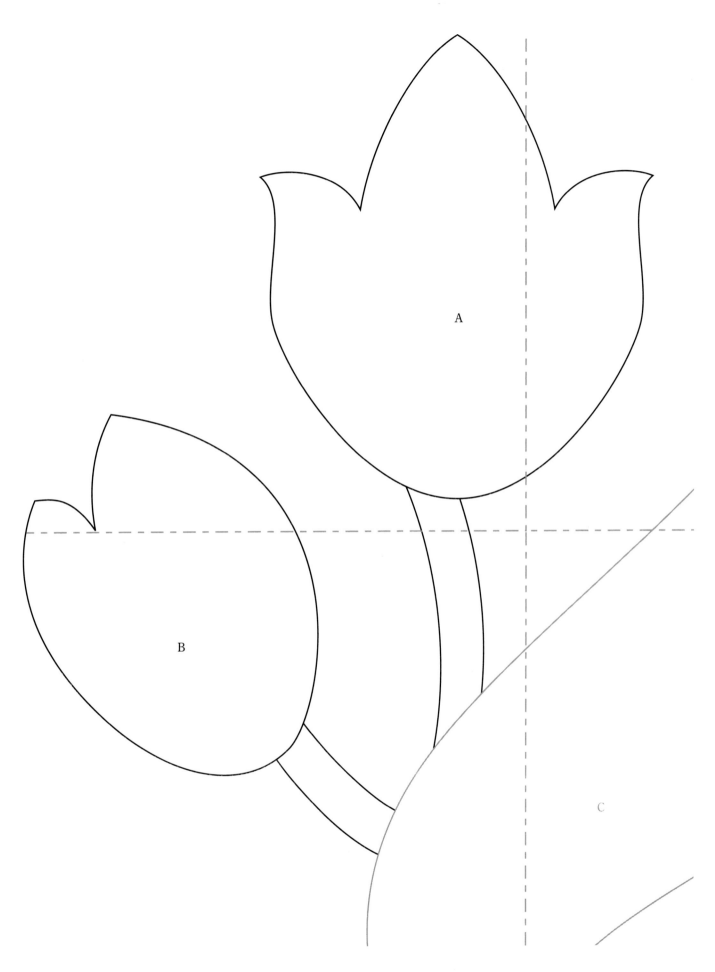

Tulip Time

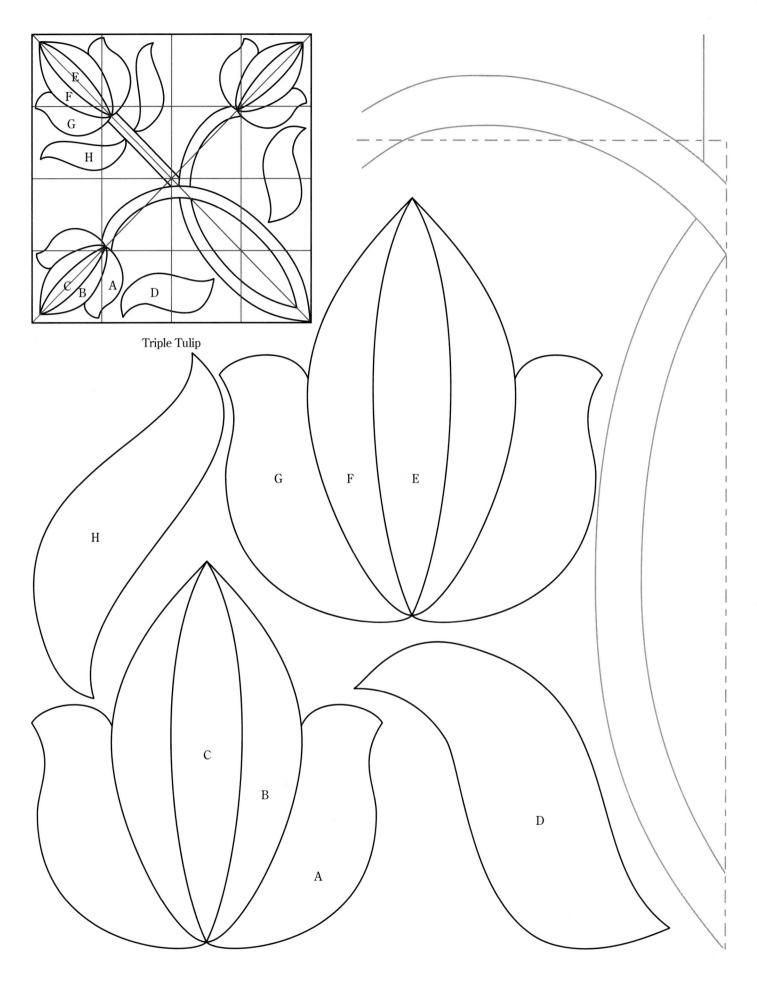

Triple Tulip

Glossary

APPLIQUE: The process of sewing one piece of fabric on top of another piece of fabric.

BACKING: The fabric which is used on the back of a quilt. Also called a lining.

BACKSTITCH: When doing the running stitch, the needle is inserted behind the thread in the previous stitch in order to lock in a line of stitching or reinforce the beginning or ending place.

BASTING: Large stitches used to temporarily hold fabric or fabrics in place.

BATTING: The filler or middle layer of a quilt.

BEARDING: The process whereby fibers from the batting find their way through to the top of the quilt.

BETWEENS: The type of needle commonly used for quilting and used by some to piece.

BINDING: The treatment given the edge of a quilt to contain the three layers.

BLOCK: A complete unit of patchwork, usually a square, which is combined with other patchwork or fabric to form a quilt.

BORDERS: Strips of fabric which can be solid, pieced or appliqued and that go completely around a unit or quilt.

CONTINUOUS LINE QUILTING: Quilting in such a manner that you can continue to quilt a design without ending the thread and starting again.

CURVED PIECING: Piecing two seams together which are curved.

DOCUMENTATION: Labeling your quilt on the back with your name, date and any other pertinent information.

FAT QUARTER: A piece of fabric that is approximately 18" x 22".

FINGER PRESSING: Creasing a sewn seam open from the right side so that one side is over both seam allowances.

JUDGED QUILT SHOW: Quilts in the show are judged and awards given.

JURIED QUILT SHOW: Quilts in the show are selected from slides or pictures of all entered quilts.

LATTICE: Strips of fabric which can be pieced, solid or appliqued which are placed between other areas or blocks of the quilt.

LINING: The back of a quilt. Also called a backing.

PIECING: Sewing pieces of fabric together to make larger units.

PRAIRIE POINTS: An edge treatment whereby small pieces of fabric are folded to form triangles which are then attached to the edge of the quilt.

QUILT AS YOU GO: Making quilted sections which are then joined to other quilted sections to complete the quilt.

QUILT CHALLENGE: Specific criteria are given to all participants in order to produce individual projects.

QUILT FRAME: Small hand held frames which hold the three layers together of a small quilted piece or larger floor frames which will hold an entire quilt for the purpose of quilting.

QUILT GUILD: A group that meets for the purpose of the preservation and enjoyment of quilting.

QUILT HOOP: Two round wooden hoops in which one hoop fits inside the other to keep the three layers together for the purpose of quilting.

QUILTING THREAD: Thread that is used for hand quilting and used by some for piecing. It will be designated as quilting thread on the spool.

ROCKER QUILTING STITCH: The running stitch when used in hand quilting.

ROTARY CUTTER: A tool which uses a round blade wheel to cut one or more pieces of fabric.

RUNNING STITCH: A line of sewing where the needle goes in and out of the fabric once for each stitch in a continuous manner.

SANDWICHING THE TOP: The process of basting the top, the batting and the backing together in preparation for hand quilting.

SASHING: Used interchangeably with the term lattice.

SEAM ALLOWANCE: The remainder of fabric beyond the stitching line, which is not seen from the right side of the fabric.

SELVAGE: The finished edge that runs lengthwise down each side of a piece of fabric.

SET ON POINT: A block which has been placed on the diagonal.

SETTING: The manner in which the blocks are placed in the quilt.

STRAIGHT: Refers to blocks set straight and placed uniformly one right after the other.

DIAGONAL: Refers to blocks set on the diagonal in a quilt.

LATTICED: Refers to the fact that the blocks whether set straight or on the diagonal have a strip of lattice between them.

SHARPS: Thin sewing needles most often used for piecing and applique.

SLEEVE or SLIP: A single or double strip of fabric attached to the back of a quilt for the purpose of sliding a pole or rod through in order to hang up the quilt.

STAB STITCH QUILTING: Process of quilting whereby one stitch at a time is taken when the needle is pushed straight down from the top of the quilt, grabbed by the hand underneath and fed back up to the top.

STENCILS: Used in order to mark the quilting designs on the top of the quilt.

STRIP or STRING QUILTING: Patchwork whereby strips of fabric are used to create the patchwork design.

TEMPLATE: The pattern that is used to mark and cut units for piecing or applique.

TIED QUILT: A quilt that is held together at regular intervals with a knotted thread, string or yarn.

Bibliography

Beyer, Jinny. *Patchwork Patterns.* McLean, VA: EPM Publications, Inc., 1979.

Beyer, Jinny. *The Quilter's Album of Blocks and Borders.* McLean, VA: EPM Publications, Inc., 1980.

Brackman, Barbara. *An Encyclopedia of Pieced Quilt Patterns.* Lawrence, KS: Prairie Flower Publishing, 1979 and 1984.

Golden, Mary. *The Friendship Quilt Book.* Dublin, NH: Yankee Books, 1985.

Gutcheon, Beth. *The Perfect Patchwork Primer.* New York: Penguin Books, 1973.

Hinson, Dolores A. *A Quilter's Companion.* New York: Arco Publishing Company, Inc., 1978.

Knoechel, Patricia. *Creating With Color.* Escondido, CA: Patricia Knoechel, 1985.

Leman, Bonnie and Martin, Judy. *Taking The Math Out of Patchwork Quilts.* Wheatridge, CO: Moon Over the Mountain Publishing Company, 1981.

Leone, Diana. *Fine Hand Quilting.* Los Altos, CA: Leone Publications, 1986.

Porter, Elizabeth and Fons, Marianne. *Classic Basket Patterns.* Atlanta, GA: Yours Truly, Inc., 1984.

Rehmel, Judy. *The Quilt I.D. Book.* New York: Prentice Hall Press, 1986.

Thompson, Shirley. *The Finishing Touch.* Edmonds, WA: Powell Publications, 1980.

Walker, Michel. *The Complete Book of Quiltmaking.* London: Edbury Press, 1985.

Quilts

FOREVER FRIENDS
Carol Doak and Sherry Reis
Center design based on a papercutting design by Alison Cosgrove Tanner

73" x 73"

WEDDING QUILT
Carol Doak
Collection of Mr. and Mrs. Joseph Drum
Queen Size

Detail of appliqued Lancaster Rose
from WEDDING QUILT.

Block frame: Calico
Blue background: Mini-print
Burgundy Leaves: Dot
White: Calico
Dark blue: Calico

SWEET SAMPLER
Carol Doak
Queen Size

Detail of Eight-Pointed Star, Evening Star, from SWEET SAMPLER.

Block frame: Combination of airy print and dot
Green background: Calico
White triangles: Solid
Center: Stripe

FINALLY QUILTING
Lori J. Ankerud
Twin Size

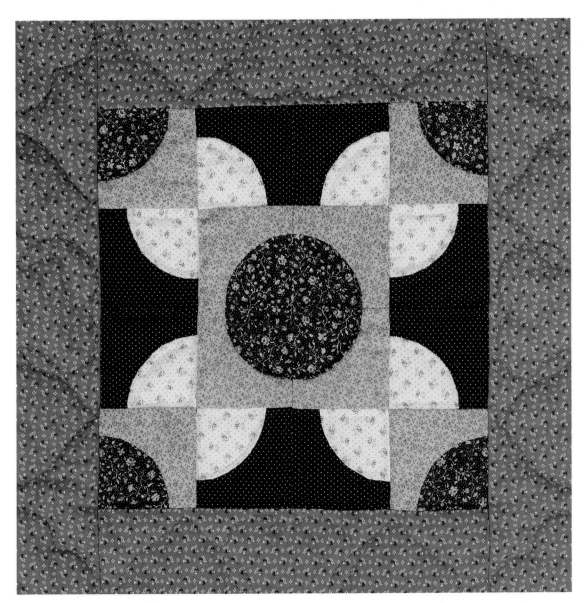

Detail of curved piecing,
Drunkard's Path variation,
from FINALLY QUILTING.

Block frame: Mini-print
Navy background: Mini-print
Center and corner navy: Calico
White: Dot
Pink: Mini-print

MINE, ALL MINE
Beth Meek
Twin Size

Detail of Nine Patch, Doves at the Feeder,
from MINE, ALL MINE.

Block frame: Mini-print
White background: Calico
Pink triangles: Mini-print
Navy square: Calico
Light Blue Square: Dot

NEVEL QUILT
Susan McDermott
Queen Size

Detail of Five Patch, Lighthouse Beacon,
from NEVEL QUILT.

Block frame: Mini-print
Pink: Mini-print
White: Calico
Light green: Calico
Center square: Solid

NANTUCKET SAMPLER
Carol Doak
Twin Size

Index

~American Quilter's Society~

dedicated to publishing books for today's quilters

The following AQS publications are currently available:

• **American Beauties: Rose & Tulip Quilts**
by Gwen Marston & Joe Cunningham
#1907: AQS, 1988, 96 pages, softbound, $14.95

• **America's Pictorial Quilts** by Caron L. Mosey
#1662: AQS, 1985, 112 pages, hardbound, $19.95

• **Applique Designs: My Mother Taught Me to Sew**
by Faye Anderson
#2121: AQS, 1990, 80 pages, softbound, $12.95

• **Arkansas Quilts: Arkansas Warmth**
Arkansas Quilter's Guild, Inc.
#1908: AQS, 1987, 144 pages, hardbound, $24.95

• **The Art of Hand Applique** by Laura Lee Fritz
#2122: AQS, 1990, 80 pages, softbound, $14.95

• **...Ask Helen More About Quilting Designs** by Helen Squire
#2099: AQS, 1990, 54 pages, 17 x 11, spiral-bound, $14.95

• **Award-Winning Quilts & Their Makers:**
The Best of AQS Shows – 1985-1987 edited by Victoria Faoro
#2207: AQS, 1991, 232 pages, softbound, $19.95

• **Classic Basket Quilts** by Elizabeth Porter and Marianne Fons
#2208: AQS, 1991, 128 pages, softbound, $16.95

• **A Collection of Favorite Quilts** by Judy Florence
#2119 AQS, 1990, 136 pages, softbound, $18.95

• **Dear Helen, Can You Tell Me?**
...all about quilting designs by Helen Squire
#1820: AQS, 1987, 56 pages, 17 x 11, spiral-bound, $12.95

• **Dyeing & Overdyeing of Cotton Fabrics** by Judy Mercer Tescher
#2030: AQS, 1990, 54 pages, softbound, $9.95

• **Flavor Quilts for Kids to Make: Complete Instructions**
for Teaching Children to Dye, Decorate & Sew Quilts
by Jennifer Amor
#2356, AQS, 1991, 120 pages., softbound, $12.95

• **Fun & Fancy Machine Quiltmaking** by Lois Smith
#1982: AQS, 1989, 144 pages, softbound, $19.95

• **Gallery of American Quilts: 1849-1988**
#1938: AQS, 1988, 128 pages, softbound, $19.95

• **Gallery of American Quilts 1860-1989: Book II**
#2129: AQS, 1990, 128 pages, softbound, $19.95

• **The Grand Finale: A Quilter's Guide to Finishing Projects**
by Linda Denner
#1924: AQS, 1988, 96 pages, softbound, $14.95

• **Heirloom Miniatures** by Tina M. Gravatt
#2097: AQS, 1990, 64 pages, softbound, $9.95

• **Home Study Course in Quiltmaking**
by Jeannie M. Spears
#2031: AQS, 1990, 240 pages, softbound, $19.95

• **Infinite Stars** by Gayle Bong
#2283: AQS, 1992, 72 pages, softbound, $12.95

• **The Ins and Outs: Perfecting the Quilting Stitch**
by Patricia J. Morris
#2120: AQS, 1990, 96 pages, softbound, $9.95

• **Irish Chain Quilts: A Workbook of Irish Chains & Related**
Patterns by Joyce B. Peaden
#1906: AQS, 1988, 96 pages, softbound, $14.95

• **Marbling Fabrics for Quilts: A Guide for Learning & Teaching**
by Kathy Fawcett and Carol Shoaf
#2206: AQS, 1991, 72 pages, softbound, $12.95

• **Missouri Heritage Quilts** by Bettina Havig
#1718: AQS, 1986, 104 pages, softbound, $14.95

• **Nancy Crow: Quilts and Influences** by Nancy Crow
#1981: AQS, 1990, 256 pages, hardcover, $29.95

• **No Dragons on My Quilt** by Jean Ray Laury with
Ritva Laury and Lizabeth Laury
#2153: AQS, 1990, 52 pages, hardcover, $12.95

• **Oklahoma Heritage Quilts** Oklahoma Quilt Heritage Project
#2032: AQS, 1990, 144 pages, softbound, $19.95

• **Quiltmaker's Guide: Basics & Beyond** by Carol Doak
#2284: AQS, 1992, 208 pages, softbound $19.95

• **QUILTS: The Permanent Collection – MAQS**
#2257: AQS, 1991, 100 pages, 10 x 6½, softbound, $9.95

• **Scarlet Ribbons: American Indian Technique for Today's Quilters**
by Helen Kelley
#1819: AQS, 1987, 104 pages, softbound, $15.95

• **Sets & Borders** by Gwen Marston and Joe Cunningham
#1821: AQS, 1987, 104 pages, softbound, $14.95

• **Somewhere in Between: Quilts and Quilters of Illinois**
by Rita Barrow Barber
#1790: AQS, 1986, 78 pages, softbound, $14.95

• **Stenciled Quilts for Christmas** by Marie Monteith Sturmer
#2098: AQS, 1990, 104 pages, softbound, $14.95

• **Texas Quilts – Texas Treasures** Texas Heritage Quilt Society
#1760: AQS, 1986, 160 pages, hardbound, $24.95

• **A Treasury of Quilting Designs** by Linda Goodmon Emery
#2029: AQS, 1990, 80 pages, 14 x 11, spiral-bound, $14.95

• **Wonderful Wearables: A Celebration of Creative Clothing**
by Virginia Avery
#2286: AQS, 1991, 168 pages, softbound, $24.95

*These books can be found in local bookstores and quilt shops. If you are unable to locate a title
in your area, you can order by mail from AQS, P.O. Box 3290, Paducah, KY 42002-3290.
Please add $1 for the first book and 40¢ for each additional one to cover postage and handling.*